NOW WHAT?

Now What?

A Guide for New
(and Not So New)
Catholics

Patrick Madrid

servant
AN IMPRINT OF
FRANCISCAN MEDIA
Cincinnati, Ohio

Cover and book design by Mark Sullivan
Cover image © istockphoto | feedough

Library of Congress Cataloging-in-Publication Data
Madrid, Patrick, 1960-
Now what? : a guide for new (and not-so-new) Catholics / Patrick Madrid.
    pages cm
ISBN 978-1-61636-721-3 (alk. paper)
1. Catholic Church—Doctrines. 2. Theology, Doctrinal—Popular works. 3. Christian life—Catholic authors. 4. Catholic Church—Customs and practices. I. Title.
BX1754.M264 2015
282—dc23
                        2014037894

ISBN 978-1-61636-721-3

Published by Servant Books, an imprint of Franciscan Media
28 W. Liberty St.
Cincinnati, OH 45202
www.FranciscanMedia.org

Printed in the United States of America.
Printed on acid-free paper.
15 16 17 18 19 5 4 3 2 1

CONTENTS

CHAPTER ONE

THE BIG PICTURE
Understand What It Means to Be Catholic

IMAGINE YOURSELF IMMIGRATING TO A DISTANT FOREIGN COUNTRY. For a long time now, you've been planning this transition, getting ready for your total immersion into another culture with exotic surroundings and languages, with laws, customs, holidays, and social conventions that differ from what you're accustomed to. Even though you're excited and ready to enthusiastically embrace this new world of ideas and experiences, you still find yourself a little apprehensive about feeling out of place once you're there. Right?

Don't worry. That feeling is totally normal. Many people feel that way as they make the journey into the Catholic Church. And for some, that feeling goes away only gradually, even after they've become Catholic. The Church is a big place filled with many wonderful things that, at first glance, might seem puzzling or difficult to get used to. In due time, these things will become familiar and comfortable. In the meantime, it helps to consult a guidebook (like this one!) to get your bearings and learn your way around.

Once you take that momentous step and officially "immigrate" into the Catholic Church, you may, understandably, find yourself asking, "Okay, now what do I do?" And while the short answer to that question is simply, "Be Catholic," it's not a terribly practical response, because those two words encompass a great deal. Let's break things down into their component parts and explore them so you can get a clear look at all the major aspects of being Catholic. This will help you see the big picture, the fifty-thousand-foot view.

Let's consider in two ways what it means to "be Catholic." First, what's involved in living out a Catholic identity? Second, what does that identity of "being Catholic" comprise? Each of these sides of the same coin deserves careful consideration.

Living as a Catholic

Being Catholic involves many rights and privileges, as well as duties and obligations, similar to the way rights and duties are part of citizenship in a given country. In the United States, for example, citizenship confers on the holder the constitutionally recognized rights to vote in elections, worship God freely, and exercise free speech, to name a few.[1] It also obligates the citizen to fulfill certain duties to the country, such as paying taxes, defending the nation by serving in the military (if drafted), and serving on a jury (if summoned).

In the same way, to be Catholic means to avail yourself of those rights and privileges that derive from your new identity as a member of the Church. In becoming Catholic, you receive God's priceless gift of grace through baptism, confirmation, and the Holy Eucharist. This transforming grace literally makes you an adopted son or daughter of God and, therefore, an heir to every good thing God has in store for those who love him. As St. Paul put it:

> For all who are led by the Spirit of God are sons of God. For you did not receive the spirit of slavery to fall back into fear, but you have received the spirit of sonship. When we cry, "Abba! Father!" it is the Spirit himself bearing witness with our spirit that we are children of God, and if children, then heirs, heirs

of God and fellow heirs with Christ, provided we suffer with him in order that we may also be glorified with him. (Romans 8:14–17)

All baptized members of the Church share in the rights and privileges that stem from that glorious status of fellow heirs with Christ. Many practical examples of this are spelled out in detail in the Church's *Code of Canon Law*[2] and include, but are not limited to:

- the right to make known your needs and desires, especially spiritual ones, to the pastors of the Church (*Canon* 212.2);
- the right to receive assistance from the pastor out of the spiritual goods of the Church, especially the Word of God and the sacraments (*Canon* 213);
- the right to participate in the mission of the Church (*Canon* 216);
- the right to be free from any kind of coercion in choosing a state in life (*Canon* 219).

Similarly, there are duties and obligations that every baptized Catholic is required to fulfill. Many of these, too, are elaborated in the *Code of Canon Law* and in the *Catechism of the Catholic Church* (see CCC 2041–2043) and include, for instance, the "Sunday obligation" (i.e., the duty to attend Mass every Sunday and every holy day of obligation[3] and to rest from all servile work on those days);[4] the obligation, if choosing marriage, to be married in the Church (unless granted a dispensation by one's bishop); the responsibility of financially supporting the work of the Church to the best of one's ability;[5] and the duty to confess your sins at least once a year and to receive the Holy Eucharist at least during the Easter season.

When you think about it, all this talk about rights and duties, although it might sound formal and legalistic, could apply to the way any family operates. Each member of a family enjoys certain privileges that come from being part of the family. And each member is expected to pull his own weight when it comes to the family's division of labor, right? Everyone, according to his age, capacity, and availability, is expected to pitch in with doing chores, yard work, and so forth. It's not that the family members are hung up on rules or anything like that. It's just that, in any human society, in order for there to be order, mutual fulfillment, and happiness, everyone involved must have certain rights and duties; we instinctively expect and respect this fact. This is no less true of the Catholic Church than it is of your own family or workplace.

Being Catholic means doing those things Catholics naturally do: going to Mass, reading the Holy Bible, praying, striving to cultivate virtue and avoid vice,[6] learning the teachings of the Church, and so forth. In short, it means living out your Catholic identity. Next, we'll consider what that identity consists of.

What Makes a Catholic

Most cradle Catholics, raised in the faith from infancy, learn the language and culture of the Church effortlessly. They speak Catholic-ese fluently and understand intuitively aspects of the Catholic Church that, for many non-Catholics, seems strange or incomprehensible, even off-putting. Examples of this are devotion to the Blessed Virgin Mary and the saints, confession to a priest, infant baptism, purgatory, and the papacy. But this is to be expected.

Anyone growing up in Spain or Germany or Japan would intuitively understand the subtle nuances of those cultures. Immigrants to those countries, however, must make an effort to understand things that are, at least at first, foreign to them. Likewise for converts, learning the language and culture of the Church is a natural and important part of becoming Catholic.

An analogy I've used many times to describe the different perspectives toward the Church is that of a stained-glass window in a large, old cathedral. When seen from the inside, as a cradle Catholic would view it, the window is bright and beautiful, an explosion of color and meaning. The light streaming through it illuminates everything. To someone looking at it from the outside—someone who was not raised in the Church—however, the same window might appear dark and dreary, lacking the color, meaning, and beauty it has when viewed from the inside. It's really a matter of perspective. And becoming Catholic involves gaining that perspective, even if it comes into view only gradually, as it tends to for most converts.

Being Catholic means embracing and assimilating into yourself the Catholic identity. It's a kind of osmosis. Recall what happens when a stalk of celery is placed upright in a glass of water and blue food coloring: It becomes entirely imbued with blue. Likewise, when you truly become Catholic, you gradually "soak up" the ethos of Catholicism, its moral and doctrinal teachings, the Mass and other liturgical celebrations, its two-thousand-year history, replete with a host of saints and martyrs, a *sensus Catholicus* (a Catholic sense of things).

To be Catholic means, as St. Paul says, "not [to] be conformed to this world but [to] be transformed by the renewal of your mind, that you may prove what is the will of God, what is good and acceptable and perfect" (Romans 12:2). That "renewal of your mind" is the perfect way to describe taking on the Catholic identity. It becomes part of you at an ever-deeper level, like the stalk of celery becoming blue from bottom to top.

The wonderful thing about all this is that membership in the Catholic Church, being universal, is not a single, monolithic, one-size-fits-all identity that everyone is forced to wear. We'd call that a straightjacket. No, our Catholic identity is expansive and many-faceted, permeated with tremendous variety and nuance. It admits some things and excludes others, the way the human body admits foods and liquids that are good for it and rejects substances that aren't. A truly Catholic identity allows a person to experience, appreciate, and cherish the profound love of God and the magnificent, even exhilarating freedom that comes with being an adopted son or daughter of God.

It is like the freedom to speak a new language without hesitating or faltering because you have learned its grammar rules and vocabulary so thoroughly that they have become part of you, second nature, right there at the tip of your tongue, so to speak, and flowing effortlessly from your mind and mouth. And let's not forget that the best way to learn to speak a language freely is to immerse yourself in it. Learn it by living and working in it, thinking in it, even dreaming in it. Once you get to that level of proficiency, you have become truly free to speak that language. 'It has become part of your identity.

Gaining a truly Catholic identity means learning to see the world in a new light—the light of Jesus Christ. What before may have been a landscape littered with objects of pleasure is now seen, in the luminous brilliance of the truth of Christ, as a path you must avoid on your journey toward your heavenly homeland; and some things that previously might have been desirable you now recognize as obstacles or snares that could trip you up and bring you down, slowing or even halting your progress toward eternal life.

In this life you now perceive great value and beauty in things that formerly you turned away from: poverty, suffering, even illness. You now understand that in the poor and lonely you behold the face of Christ. And in difficulties such as illness you see the means for you to do as Christ bade you: to take up your cross and follow him all the way to heaven.

Having a Catholic identity means, ultimately, to become conformed to the likeness of Jesus Christ (see Romans 8:29) so that you "may know him and the power of his resurrection, and may share his sufferings, becoming like him in his death [i.e., victorious over death and sin] that if possible [you] may attain the resurrection from the dead. Not that [you] have already obtained this or [are] already perfect; but [you] press on to make it [your] own, because Christ Jesus has made [you] his own" (Philippians 3:10–12).

You'll know that you are gaining a truly Catholic identity when, like that stalk of celery soaking up the food coloring, you start to forget "what lies behind and [strain] forward to what lies ahead…[pressing] on toward the goal for the prize of the upward call of God in Christ Jesus" (see Philippians 3:13–14).

OVERCOMING OBSTACLES TO GAINING A CATHOLIC IDENTITY

Some of the more common challenges new Catholics face when it comes to acquiring, broadening, and deepening an authentically Catholic identity are:

- complacency (aka, laziness or lukewarmness);
- the triumph of the imagination over the intellect;
- other Catholics;
- fear of truth.

To use a maritime analogy, the first obstacle, complacency, is like the state of a ship becalmed in a still ocean with no breeze. The wind has gone out of its sails, and it makes no forward progress. It just sits there. It's important to invoke the Holy Spirit's help continually, especially in moments when you no longer feel the initial joy and euphoria that often accompanies one's entrance into the Church. The Holy Spirit will put the wind back into your sails if you ask him to. For, as St. Paul says, "The Spirit helps us in our weakness; for we do not know how to pray as we ought, but the Spirit himself intercedes for us with sighs too deep for words" (Romans 8:26).

The second obstacle, imagination over intellect, can be illustrated by a ship's captain who sails toward his destination relying only on his intuition, or a hunch, rather than using maps, a compass, and a sextant. He steers the ship toward wherever he *feels* his home port should be but never consults his charts or navigational instruments. The likelihood of his ever actually arriving at his destination is pretty slim. A similar problem lurks in the background for Catholics and can get them off course—perhaps even way off course—if they're not alert to it.

The problem is not your imagination (i.e., a faculty of your soul that creates mental images based on things your senses have experienced).[7] That's something God gave you as part of your human nature. We need our faculty of imagination to think about things we experience. The problem is when someone relies exclusively on the mental images his imagination produces and never makes the effort to apply his intellect to better understand deeper truths that cannot be imagined.

Take, for example, the doctrine of the Blessed Trinity. This truth simply cannot be adequately imagined because, in this life, your bodily senses of sight, touch, hearing, and so forth have never (and can never) encounter the reality of one God in three persons. You've never seen that or anything like that, so your imagination cannot create a mental image of it for you to think about. At best, your imagination can picture a scene such as an old, white-bearded man (God the Father) seated next to a young, dark-haired Jesus (the Son) with a dove (the Holy Spirit) hovering above them. No doubt, you've seen such depictions of the Trinity countless times. It is perhaps the most universal attempt by human beings to imagine what God in his Trinitarian inner life might look like. But, of course, that is not what the Trinity actually looks like.

We have to do the best we can with our limited human imaginations.

Okay, so here's where the difficulty comes in: Some people lapse into a kind of intellectual laziness about these deep truths and simply poke along at the level of the mental images their imaginations create for them, never bothering to exercise their intellectual muscles to think about and thereby comprehend those truths more deeply. This is one reason I encourage Catholics and others to read Frank Sheed's superb books *Theology for Beginners* and *Theology and Sanity* (read them in that order, by the way, for the latter builds upon the former). Sheed does an excellent job of helping the reader move beyond the shallow "wading pool" of mere imagination into the deeper and immensely more beautiful and inspiring ocean of truth about God. He essentially shows you how to swim out into those deeper waters so that you can learn far more than what your finite imagination can provide.

One final thought here about the cramped limitations of human imagination. Another difficulty arises when, because someone can't imagine a given truth, he decides it can't be true. Case in point: I have met more than a few Jehovah's Witnesses who have explained to me that they reject the divinity of Jesus Christ because they can't "picture" (i.e., imagine) how he could be true God and true man, 100 percent divine and 100 percent human, in what Catholics call the "hypostatic union."

They're right, of course, that we strain to the absolute limits of human ability to imagine such a wondrous reality, but the fact that we can't imagine it does not in the slightest make it untrue. One Jehovah's Witness who visited my home told me very sincerely, "I just can't believe in the Trinity because I can't imagine how there could be one God in three persons. It just doesn't make sense to me." As you might imagine, I did my best to help her look at this divine mystery through reason aided by divine revelation, without resorting to mental images, but I never knew if it was helpful to her because she left soon thereafter and never came back. I wish I had given her Sheed's *Theology for Beginners*.

The third obstacle I'd like to warn you about—other Catholics—can be compared to rocky shoals that lie just out of sight below the surface of the water. The problem is really pretty simple: Sometimes new Catholics become scandalized by the apathy, misbehavior, meanness, or hypocrisy they see in their fellow Catholics, and this can have a very demoralizing effect. Don't let that get you down!

First of all, don't forget that you're a sinner, too, and we all carry crosses and burdens that can make us, shall we say, less than delightful to be around sometimes.

Just as you wouldn't stop trying to live healthfully, exercise, and eat right just because you saw a fat, chain-smoking, out-of-shape cardiologist, you should not be deterred in your desire to live the Catholic faith to the fullest just because you encounter some Catholics who aren't doing that. And besides, the Catholic Church is like a big hospital for people who are afflicted with the sickness of sin. That's why Christ established the Catholic Church in the first place! It's there that he dispenses to us those cures for what ails us, especially in the Mass, in the Eucharist and the other sacraments, in the Holy Bible, and in so many other ways.

Bottom line: Don't let other Catholics get you down. You can safely assume that most are good, sincere people who love God and are trying to cooperate with his grace in their lives. And even when you run into someone who doesn't come across that way, treat him or her with respect and patience, the way you'd want others to treat you, and move forward. If you do your best to be a good witness of Christian joy to those around you, showing good example to them by your charitable and amiable disposition, you can help them become better. This is a big part of what St. Paul meant when he said, "Bear one another's burdens, and so fulfill the law of Christ" (Galatians 6:2).

By the fourth obstacle, fear of truth, I mean our natural human tendency to shy away from certain truths that, once we know them, will obligate us to change our ways. Think, for example, of an alcoholic who lives in denial about her drinking problem, using all kinds of rationalizations and excuses for why she doesn't need to stop drinking, although her life is crumbling around her as a result of it. She doesn't want to face the truth because doing so would mean she'd have to stop drinking. And she doesn't want to stop. So, until she hits rock bottom or her family and friends try an intervention to get her attention, she bumps along, telling herself everything's fine, when she knows it's really not. That kind of denial can be fatal in the long run.

And there's an analogous type of denial in the Christian life, too, that happens when one decides which teachings of the Church he'd rather ignore because, if he faced up to them and acknowledged their truth, he would have to change his lifestyle. This is very common, for example, when it comes to the Catholic Church's teaching that artificial contraception is seriously immoral, bad for women, bad for men, bad for marriages, and ultimately, bad for one's relationship with God.[8] As the late, great Archbishop Fulton Sheen used to say, "It's easy to find the truth. It's hard to face it; and harder still to follow it." But let's never forget that, as Jesus himself said, "You will know the truth and the truth will set you free" (John 8:32, *NAB*).

Plato's famous Allegory of the Cave[9] is a helpful way to think about what it means to be Catholic and to embrace the truth, even when (especially when) it means having to change something in your own life in order to do so.

The ancient philosopher describes a hypothetical cave in which people are imprisoned and are forced to sit and watch shadows cast onto the back wall by others who, completely unseen, stand above and behind them, projecting the images of people, animals, and so forth, "made out of stone, wood, and every material," using light from a bonfire. The sounds of their voices as they cast the shadows gives the impression that the shadows themselves can speak. This causes the captive audience to assume that the images they see on the wall are real, because they can see and hear them.

Plato says, "The prisoners would in every way believe that the truth is nothing other than the shadows of those artifacts." This is perfectly reasonable, of course, because these shadow pictures are all the captives have ever known about "reality." They have no idea that the real world exists just beyond the cave in which they are confined.

Speaking to his interlocutor, a colleague named Glaucon, Plato continues:

> "Consider, then, what being released from their bonds and cured of their ignorance would naturally be like, if something like this came to pass. When one of them was freed and suddenly compelled to stand up, turn his head, walk, and look up toward the light, he'd be pained and dazzled and unable to see the things whose shadows he'd seen before. What do you think he'd say, if we told him what he'd seen before was inconsequential, but that now—because he is a bit closer to the things that are [i.e., real things] and is turned toward things that are more—he sees more correctly? Or, to put it another way, if we pointed to each of the things passing by, asked him what each of them is, and compelled him to answer, don't you think he'd be at a loss and that he'd believe that the things he saw earlier were truer than the things he was now being shown?"
>
> "Much truer," Glaucon responds.
>
> "And if someone compelled him to look at the light itself, wouldn't his eyes hurt, and wouldn't he turn around and flee

towards the things he is able to see, believing that they are really clearer than the ones he's being shown?"

"He would."

"And if someone dragged him away from there by force, up the rough, steep path, and didn't let him go until he had dragged him into the sunlight, wouldn't he be pained and irritated at being treated that way? And when he came into the light, with the sun filling his eyes, wouldn't he be unable to see a single one of the things now said to be true?"

"He would be unable to see them, at least at first."

"I suppose, then, that he'd need time to get adjusted before he could see things in the world above. At first, he'd see shadows most easily, then images of men and other things in water [i.e., reflected in water], then the things themselves. Of these, he'd be able to study the things in the sky and the sky itself more easily at night, looking at the light of the stars and the moon, than during the day, looking at the sun and the light of the sun."

"Of course."[10]

All of us are like those people in Plato's Cave. We must strive to overcome various limitations, ignorance, prejudices, and preconceived ideas we may have grown up with or picked up along the way, "blind spots" that prevent us from knowing more fully truths about God and the world around us.

The earliest example of this that I can remember in my own life was when I discovered, at about age five, that not everyone in the world was Catholic. I had just assumed that everyone was Catholic because it had never entered my little mind that anything else was possible. At that young age, I had no reason to doubt anything my parents had taught me about Jesus, Mary, the Mass, or the Bible. I had a childlike faith then (as we all did at one time) and simply accepted what they taught me at face value. So, it puzzled me that not everyone was Catholic and that some people did not believe in what I had been taught to be true.

It's an amusing notion, but it came as a shock to me then. As I grew older, I continued to have my assumptions challenged. Some were corrected with truths previously unknown to me, and some (for example, that God exists and he loves me) were confirmed as in fact true.

Each time we grapple with elements of reality by making an honest effort to understand and come to terms with them, we come out of that cave a little bit more, into the shining light of truth. As Plato points out, though, the truth can often be difficult to behold and even more difficult to accept and embrace. We see an example of this in John, chapter 6, where Jesus begins to reveal the doctrine of his real presence in the Holy Eucharist.

> "I am the living bread which came down from heaven; if any one eats of this bread, he will live for ever; and the bread which I shall give for the life of the world is my flesh."
>
> The Jews then disputed among themselves, saying, "How can this man give us his flesh to eat?"
>
> So Jesus said to them, "Truly, truly, I say to you, unless you eat the flesh of the Son of man and drink his blood, you have no life in you; he who eats my flesh and drinks my blood has eternal life, and I will raise him up at the last day. For my flesh is food indeed, and my blood is drink indeed. He who eats my flesh and drinks my blood abides in me, and I in him." (John 6:51–56)

But this truth was simply too much for some of the Lord's disciples, many of whom "drew back and no longer went about with him" (John 6:66). Let this be a cautionary tale for the rest of us.

Not every truth is easy to understand or, more importantly, easy to follow. Take, for example, Christ's commands to love and forgive enemies and to do good to those who persecute you (see Matthew 5:44; Luke 6:27). Talk about easier said than done! Or what about his teaching that "everyone who looks at a woman lustfully has already committed adultery with her in his heart"? (Matthew 5:28). The fact is, these truths and many others like them can be exceedingly difficult to adhere to without God's grace (see Psalm 86:5–7).

And then there are those truths that our intellects have great difficulty understanding. These include doctrines such as the Trinity (how can there be one God in three divine persons?),[11] the hypostatic union (how can Jesus be true God and true man?), and the omnipotence and love of God (if God is all-powerful and all-loving, then why does he permit evil and suffering?).[12]

The more deeply we come to know Jesus Christ, who is "the way, the truth, and the life" (John 14:6), the more we can accommodate the truth. Jesus wants to draw us into the fullness of truth because, as he said, "the truth will set you free" (John 8:32, *NAB*).

To become Catholic—whether as a convert or as a cradle Catholic who begins with an immature or childish faith and develops a mature, informed faith based on conviction—means to enter into the truth. The problem is that we typically don't realize we're in the cave in the first place! Those things we once thought were true sometimes turn out to be something less.

RCIA

Becoming Catholic is a process that begins, for most people, with a period of prayer, study, and spiritual preparation known in the United States as the Rite of Christian Initiation of Adults (RCIA). Here is an overview of that process.

This first step in a convert's journey into the Catholic Church is to respond to Christ's invitation to "come and see":

> Jesus turned, and saw them following, and said to them, "What do you seek?" And they said to him, "Rabbi" (which means Teacher), "where are you staying?" He said to them, "Come and see." They came and saw where he was staying; and they stayed with him that day. (John 1:38–39)

Our initial curiosity to know more about Jesus Christ is fed and strengthened as the Church provides inquirers with an introduction to the Good News and a comprehensive explanation of the teachings and customs of the Church, including doctrines such as the Blessed Trinity (i.e., one God in three persons), the Incarnation of Jesus Christ (i.e., the Son of God becoming man), the atonement (i.e., that Jesus suffered and died on the Cross for our redemption and salvation), and the Holy Eucharist (i.e., that Jesus is truly present, body, blood, soul, and divinity, under the appearances of bread and wine). Catholic customs (which we will explore in more depth later in this book) include such things as calling priests "father," the liturgical calendar, sacramentals (e.g., holy water, candles, medals, incense, the sign of the cross), and forms of Catholic spirituality and piety (e.g., Eucharistic Adoration, praying the Rosary, reading the Holy Bible).

In the next phase of this process, the inquirer is formally welcomed into the parish where he or she is taking RCIA classes. This is known as the time of *catechumenate*, and those who are now officially on the journey into the Church are called "catechumens," from the Greek word *katēcheō* (κατηχέω), which means both "one who is taught" and "one who teaches" (the catechist). St. Paul uses these terms in Galatians 6:6, where he says, "Let him who is taught the word share all good things with him who teaches" (see also Luke 1:4; Acts 18:24; 1 Corinthians 4:19). This time of preparing spiritually and mentally to be formally received into the Church has its roots in Christ's command to the apostles to "make disciples" of all people (Matthew 28:19). The apostles were the Church's very first catechists, going forth on their worldwide mission to carry out Christ's mandate to teach "them to observe all that I have commanded" (Matthew 28:20). And a disciple is one who not only follows after the Master but learns everything he can about his teachings and seeks to live according to them.

Eventually, catechumens experience the Church's Rite of Election, in which they prepare in earnest for being formally received into the Church. They are now known in the Church as the Elect (i.e., "chosen") for, as Jesus said: "You did not choose me, but I chose you and appointed you that you should go and bear fruit and that your fruit should abide; so that whatever you ask the Father in my name, he may give it to you" (John 15:16).

During these remaining weeks, the Elect are exhorted to deepen and intensify their preparation through prayer and study so that, when they reach the summit of their journey on Holy Saturday Night, at the Easter Vigil Mass, they will be properly disposed to enter into these great mysteries of Christ's life, death, and resurrection in the sacraments of the Church.

At the Easter Vigil Mass, the Elect make a formal renunciation of sin, a renewal of their baptismal promises (in the case of those who have already been baptized), a public profession of faith ("I believe and profess all that the holy Catholic Church believes, teaches, and proclaims to be revealed by God"), and then receiving the sacraments of initiation: baptism, the Holy Eucharist, and confirmation. (Those who have already been validly baptized receive the initiating sacraments of the Holy Eucharist and confirmation.)

Because of the power of Jesus Christ working in these sacraments so that they actually do what they symbolize, one's new identity as a Catholic, fully incorporated now into the body of Christ, the Church, is made real and indelible.

For some converts, what happens next can seem very anticlimactic. They have been through the long buildup of the *catechumenate* program culminating in the profoundly beautiful, even majestic, experience of the Easter Vigil Mass, during which they have been formally received into the Church. And then, once they're "in" the Church and the special attention they received leading up to their entrance begins to fade into memory, they are expected to take their rightful places in the life of the Church and live out their Catholic identity. This is where it can become perplexing and even, for some, discouraging, as they see even more clearly that to be Catholic means to experience a wide range of realties, some of which can seem mundane while others are deeply meaningful.

But it's really just like living in any family. True, there are joyful holiday get-togethers, birthday celebrations, and special events that punctuate the year with happy times and opportunities to renew love and friendships, but there are also many more unexciting things such as household chores, yard work, errands, and the like that are also part of—a big part of—normal family life. The same is true for life in the Catholic Church. We're a big family.

St. Paul also uses the metaphor of the Church as the body of Christ: "For just as the body is one and has many members, and all the members of the body, though many, are one body, so it is with Christ" (1 Corinthians 12:12). We all know from experience that family life, for all its happiness and occasional moments of great joy, can also be difficult, especially insofar as we must get along with each other and put up with the personality quirks and shortcomings that we all have. This is certainly true in the Catholic Church. It is a divine institution made up of weak human members, and this is why you'll soon discover that it can be rather untidy and its members a bit unruly at times. But that's okay. This is the Church Jesus Christ established, and because it is *his* Church, he selects the materials he wishes to use to build it.

The Holy Bible says that we ourselves are that material. "Like living stones, be yourselves built into a spiritual house, to be a holy priesthood, to offer spiritual sacrifices acceptable to God through Jesus Christ" (1 Peter 2:5). It shouldn't surprise us, then, to find that the Church's imperfect, sinful human members—we who are the "living stones" Jesus has chosen to build with—have plenty of rough edges and ragged contours that require a great deal of shaping, smoothing, and polishing by the Lord's hammer and chisel of grace so that they can each fit perfectly into the places he has chosen for us.

THE CHURCH IS UNIVERSAL

You've no doubt heard that the word Catholic means "universal." This is true. The Greek word *katholikos* (καθολικός) derives from the phrase "for the whole" (*katá hólos*, κατά όλος), which we can see expressed in the Great Commission, when Jesus commands the apostles to go forth into the whole world and make disciples of "all nations" (see Matthew 2:19–20). This means that the Good News of salvation and the Lord's invitation to enter the Church is for all people in all places at all times.

The Catholic Church is universal in that it reaches out to everyone everywhere. It's not a Church just for a certain race or social class or geographical area. As St. Paul said, "There is neither Jew nor Greek, there is neither slave nor free, there is neither male nor female; for you are all one in Christ Jesus" (Galatians 3:28). Nor is the Catholic Church a "national church," primarily associated with a particular country or culture (e.g., Russian, Greek, Chinese, Mexican). Rather, it transcends all national boundaries and cultural peculiarities, embracing the entire human family. The Catholic Church "tests all things" in all cultures, so that it can "hold fast what is good" (1 Thessalonians 5:21).

A FINAL THOUGHT

While becoming Catholic is a pretty straightforward process, the life-long project of being Catholic can be joy-filled and inspiring at times, just as, at times, it can be trying and difficult. It's like the weather. There are sunny days and cloudy days. But the clouds will pass in due time. And, as you know, the sun (God) has not gone away, even on those days when you can't see it (him) for the clouds.

Sometimes, your emotions will get the better of you, and you may grow disgusted with your fellow Catholics or with circumstances you encounter in the Catholic Church and become tempted (even if ever so slightly) to throw in the towel. Don't. Remember, the Catholic Church is similar to Noah's ark. Like the ark, it can be a muddled, tumultuous place because of its unruly passengers. But when the floodwaters begin to cut loose, one's options are very simple: You can either get on board the ark, deal with the commotion, and ride out the storm in safety, or you can decline to get on board and take your chances. Becoming Catholic is the equivalent of choosing the first option.

CHAPTER TWO

FEAST OR FAMINE

Get the Most Out of the Mass and the Sacraments

THE HEART OF EVERY FAMILY CELEBRATION IS FOOD, RIGHT? TRY TO imagine celebrating Christmas or Thanksgiving without food! No matter what one's customary holiday fare might be, no one can deny that food greatly enriches and enlivens these gatherings.

In every culture and in all ages, special feasts prepared for holidays, birthdays, weddings, and even funerals. They are integral to the rhythm of life. Food is integral to life. God made it that way. We are not like angels who, being pure spirits with no bodies, have no need for food. Nor are we in this way like animals, which have no rational souls and, therefore, are unable to perceive meaning in events and occasions. Animals simply eat according to the dictates of instinct and necessity, not for enjoyment or to "celebrate" or "commemorate" anything. They have no capacity for such things.

Human beings, on the other hand, inhabit both the supernatural realm of pure spirit and the physical realm of matter and space. We are *composite* beings composed of bodies and souls. You are not merely a soul in a body (like a hand in a glove), or merely a body with a soul inside (like a computer with software loaded into it). As a human being, you are an integrated, body-and-soul whole. And your body and soul are designed by God to be united for all eternity.[1]

Just as physical food nourishes the body, the spiritual food of the Holy Eucharist is a banquet given to us by God to nourish and strengthen our souls as we make our way homeward to heaven. It is also the family meal that all of his children are invited to attend and partake in, something echoed in the priest's words at the *Agnus Dei* (Lamb of God) prayer at Mass: "Behold the Lamb of God, behold him who takes away the sins of the world. Blessed are those called to the supper of the Lamb."

Our response to that prayer—"Lord, I am not worthy that you should enter under my roof, but only say the word and my soul shall be healed"—reminds us that this great gift of Christ's presence among his people in the humble form of food is something we are not worthy to have, and yet the Lord in his love comes to us in this Eucharistic bread to heal and invigorate us.

Now that you're Catholic, or considering becoming Catholic, it is very important for you to understand the immense importance of the Mass and the Holy Eucharist. Chances are you already have a clear understanding of the Catholic Church's teaching that Jesus Christ is truly present in the Blessed Sacrament (the real presence) and that it's at the Mass that this miracle of transubstantiation takes place (more about that term in a moment). In this chapter, we'll consider a few crucial aspects of this teaching that will help you dive even deeper into the ocean of the Lord's unfathomable love for you.

Like the Israelites who wandered in the desert for forty years before entering the Promised Land, members of the body of Christ (also known as the Church militant) who are still in this life require food for the journey to heaven. God miraculously provided food for the Israelites, in the form of manna and quail (see Exodus 16), particularly in those times when they were weak, afraid, and discouraged. This food strengthened and encouraged them to press onward toward their goal. Similarly, though supernaturally and with awesome spiritual power, he does the same for his people through the sacraments.

This is why, as Jesus began to teach the Jews of his day about the Eucharist, he made the connection between the manna and the Eucharist explicit:

> So they said to him, "Then what sign do you do, that we may see, and believe you? What work do you perform? Our fathers ate the manna in the wilderness; as it is written, 'He gave them bread from heaven to eat.'" Jesus then said to them, "Truly, truly, I say to you, it was not Moses who gave you the bread from heaven; my Father gives you the true bread from heaven. For the bread of God is that which comes down from heaven, and gives life to the world."
>
> They said to him, "Lord, give us this bread always."
>
> Jesus said to them, "I am the bread of life; he who comes to me shall not hunger, and he who believes in me shall never thirst." (John 6:30–35)

The Holy Eucharist—the ultimate "soul food"—is, like each of the other sacraments, God's special means of supplying what we need to make our journey to heaven. We get hungry and weary along the way, and sometimes, when we fall and injure ourselves through sin or wander off and become lost and emaciated through starvation, we need the healing properties this spiritual food of the sacraments provides.

Breaking Bread Together

The phrase, "breaking bread together" means more than just grabbing a quick bite to stave off hunger. That phrase connotes a deeper significance of two or more people sharing something that transcends the mere consumption of food. We all feel this unspoken meaning intuitively at a primal level because, as experience shows, we enjoy deeper satisfaction and happiness when we savor food with others.

It is here, then, that we can begin to understand why the Lord Jesus Christ endowed the Church with the gift of sacraments. They are, in a sense, the spiritual "food" for the soul that mediates grace to us through our contact with certain physical elements, such as bread, wine, water, and oil.

Through the sacraments, God's global family, the Church, gathers to enjoy our sacred and saving family meal which Jesus Christ prepared for us by his life, atoning death on the Cross, and resurrection. Beginning with the Eucharist that comes to us from the Mass, all the sacraments, each in its own way, feed us.

Signs, Signs, Everywhere

We live in a world of signs. They point toward and signify other things, things that exist even though we may not see them. We take signs for granted because we are so accustomed to them, but we still understand instinctively the difference between a sign and what it points to.

For example, consider the word *lasagna*. Those few squiggles have meaning because they signify the reality of a tasty dish you've no doubt enjoyed many times. The word-symbol *lasagna* (all written and spoken words are symbols) automatically evokes in your imagination a nice steaming plate of the pasta casserole. You can picture what it looks like, its aroma, what it tastes like. That's how signs and symbols work.

Consider these other examples of signs:

- Your cell phone vibrates when someone calls you—the ring and vibration point toward the reality that someone wants to communicate with you.
- The needle on the gas tank indicator on your car's dashboard dips down into the red zone—it's pointing toward the unseen reality that you're nearly out of fuel.
- Red flashing lights indicate danger. Sirens indicate an emergency. Smoke rising in the distance indicates a fire.

- The wedding band on a woman's finger is an outward sign of the inward reality that she is married.
- The shape of a heart your husband or wife traces on a steamy bathroom mirror needs no explanation.

The sacraments are, as the *Baltimore Catechism* puts it, "outward signs instituted by Christ to give grace," and, as St. Thomas Aquinas tells us, they "derive their efficacy from the Word Incarnate Himself."[2] They are signs, but not merely signs: they accomplish the realities toward which they point: cleansing, healing, feeding, strengthening, uniting, setting apart, and so on. For example, baptism symbolizes cleansing and actually does cleanse us from original sin. But it does more: It is also an "appeal to God for a clear conscience through the resurrection of Jesus Christ" (1 Peter 3:21).

The sacraments, as signs instituted by Christ to give grace, have two important parts, known as "form" and "matter." Both are required for the sacrament to be valid (more on validity in a moment).

Form refers to the *formula* by which the sacrament is conferred. For example, the form of the sacrament of baptism is the pouring of water over the head (or total immersion in water) as the one baptizing audibly speaks the words: "I baptize you in the name of the Father, and of the Son, and of the Holy Spirit." The matter of baptism is water. It must be actual water, not root beer, wine, or motor oil.

The form of the sacrament of confession (also called reconciliation or penance) is, after the penitent confesses his sins, the priest's pronouncing the words: "I absolve you from your sins in the name of the Father, and of the Son, and of the Holy Spirit." The matter of confession is the sins that are confessed.

The form of the Eucharist are the words of consecration spoken by the priest over the bread: "This is my body which will be given up for you," and over the wine, "This is the chalice of my blood, the blood of the new and eternal covenant, which will be poured out for you and for many for the forgiveness of sins." The matter of the Eucharist is bread and wine.

In the Great Commission, when Jesus sends the apostles out into the world to "make disciples of all men," he says that the entrance into the Catholic Church he had just established was through the doorway of the sacrament of baptism. "[Baptize] them," he told them, "in the name of the Father and of the Son and of the Holy Spirit" (Matthew 28:19).

This is an important biblical clue about the nature of the Church and its mission to the world. It is a sacramental Church, endowed by Christ with special graces and power (his power) to help us follow him even when the storms of life make that difficult.

True, the Lord could have sent the Church forth without any sacraments, with just the Bible (some people think this is what he did), but there's a reason why he didn't. An analogy I've found particularly helpful in explaining this is that of an orchestra:

Orchestras are formed for a single purpose: to play music. It would do no good to establish an orchestra, a group of trained musicians, if you didn't provide them with musical instruments with which to make music, right? Can you imagine the absurdity of an orchestra gathering in a concert hall, with a large audience in attendance, if the only thing those instrument-less members of the orchestra could do was *describe* music to their listeners? How ridiculous! The audience is there to hear and see music performed. Offering no more than a lecture about how pleasant the music would sound, *if only it were played,* utterly defeats the purpose of forming an orchestra. Musicians play music; they don't describe it. People want to *hear* music, not mere descriptions of what music sounds like.

So it is with the Catholic Church. It is the orchestra. The Mass is the spiritual equivalent of the musical instruments. And the Holy Eucharist is the music the orchestra plays. In other words, it would not be good enough for Jesus if his followers could do nothing but go into the whole world and tell others about who he is. Don't get me wrong! That is very good and necessary in itself, to be sure. But even better than the Church's telling people about Jesus, describing him to them, recounting his life story and teachings to everyone—all of which is good and necessary—even better than that is introducing people to Jesus Christ himself. This is precisely what Jesus has empowered the Catholic Church to do through the Mass and the Holy Eucharist.

What musical instruments are to an orchestra, the Mass is to the Church. And what music itself is to the audience, the Holy Eucharist is to all who enter the Catholic Church and thus partake of it. They are really receiving Jesus, body, blood, soul, and divinity (in other words, the glorified, risen Christ) under the appearances of bread and wine.

Simply put, as a Catholic, you can rejoice and thank God that you can have the most personal relationship with Jesus humanly possible in this earthly life. You not only can hear about him in sermons, read about him in the Holy Bible, learn his doctrines and come to love him with all your heart, mind, and strength, but—greater than all those things combined—you are able to receive him into your very body when you receive Holy Communion. That is the personal relationship that Christ wants to have with you.[3]

In becoming Catholic, you receive the greatest of all gifts in receiving the Lord in the Holy Eucharist. Don't underestimate or neglect this treasure, and, by all means, resist temptations toward apathy and complacency about this gift of Mass and the Eucharist. Always think of going to Mass as an opportunity, not as merely an obligation.

SUNDAY MASS

One of the duties all Catholics have—really, a noble privilege—is to attend Mass every Sunday. (To vote in elections is similarly both a duty and a privilege for every citizen.) Going to Sunday Mass is the best way to participate fully in the life of the Church, the body of Christ, and since time immemorial, the Church has always emphasized how important it is to fulfill this obligation to God, to the rest of the Church, and to yourself.

The apostles and the earliest Christians observed the Third Commandment, to keep holy the Lord's Day, by celebrating not on the Sabbath, as the Jews did, but on "the Lord's Day," Sunday (Acts 20:7; 1 Corinthians 16:2). This was primarily because Sunday was the day of the Lord's resurrection (see Matthew 28:1–6; John 20:1). It was also a way to draw a distinction between Christianity and Judaism, to emphasize that the one comes from the other and that all the old things and temporary legal requirements, such as observing the kosher food laws, animal sacrifices, Sabbath days, and so forth, had passed away and were now fulfilled in Christ (see Colossians 3:16–17). Those Mosaic ceremonial precepts and commandments were merely "types and shadows of heavenly realities" (see Hebrews 8:5, 10:1), those perfect things that were given by Christ in the New Covenant.

One very early monument to the apostolic tradition of Mass on Sunday is found in the *Didache*, a collection of teachings of the twelve apostles (composed about A.D. 100), which includes the rule to "gather together on the Lord's Day." By the year 155, St. Justin Martyr wrote that this practice was universal among Catholics.

In the words of St. John Paul II:

> What began as a spontaneous practice later became a juridically sanctioned norm. The Lord's Day has structured the

history of the Church through two thousand years: How could we think that it will not continue to shape her future?

The pressures of today can make it harder to fulfill the Sunday obligation; and, with a mother's sensitivity, the Church looks to the circumstances of each of her children. In particular, she feels herself called to a new catechetical and pastoral commitment, in order to ensure that, in the normal course of life, none of her children are deprived of the rich outpouring of grace which the celebration of the Lord's Day brings....

Given its many meanings and aspects, and its link to the very foundations of the faith, the celebration of the Christian Sunday remains, on the threshold of the Third Millennium, an indispensable element of our Christian identity.[4]

Partaking of the Eucharist Unworthily

Before we move forward to a biblical overview of the seven sacraments, let's pause to consider one particularly delicate aspect of the Holy Eucharist that you should understand, especially as it may affect your non-Catholic friends and loved ones. It also affects Catholics, though for a different reason.

No doubt you've experienced or at least heard about situations in which non-Catholic family members or friends graciously attend Mass—say, for a Catholic wedding or funeral—only to discover that they are not permitted by the Catholic Church to receive Holy Communion. This is vexing and off-putting to many because they feel it's exclusionary and condescending.

"Why can't I receive Communion in the Catholic Church?" your brother-in-law Rick asks, offended. "Catholics are allowed to receive Communion in my nondenominational church. What's the big deal? And why would the Catholic Church block people from receiving if, as it teaches, it's really Jesus?"

This kind of perplexity is understandable and, by way of an answer, I'll explain the Catholic Church's very good reason for this policy.

First, remember that the Holy Eucharist is the very body and blood, soul and divinity of Jesus under the appearances of bread and wine. This is what we mean in the Catholic Church by the *Real Presence*.

As the *Catechism* explains:

> The mode of Christ's presence under the eucharistic species is unique. It raises the Eucharist above all the sacraments as "the perfection of the spiritual life and the end to which all the sacraments tend." In the most blessed sacrament of the Eucharist "the body and blood, together with the soul and divinity, of our Lord Jesus Christ and, therefore, the whole Christ is truly, really, and substantially contained." "This presence is called 'real'—by which is not intended to exclude the other types of presence as if they could not be 'real' too, but because it is presence in the fullest sense: that is to say, it is a substantial presence by which Christ, God and man, makes himself wholly and entirely present." (*CCC* 1374)

Virtually no Protestant denominations hold that Jesus is truly present in their communion,[5] teaching instead that the bread they use is just bread and does not change, and the wine, grape juice, or water they use is just that and likewise does not change.

The Catholic Church doesn't argue with any of this. In fact, in order for the miracle of transubstantiation to occur in the first place, there must be present a validly ordained priest who can "confect" (i.e., prepare or cause to come into existence) the Eucharistic bread and wine. He must have validly received the sacrament of holy orders. Protestant ministers neither have nor claim to have valid holy orders (primarily because most deny the existence of this sacrament in the first place), so to them this is really a moot point.

Thus, the reason the Catholic Church does not permit non-Catholics to receive Holy Communion is based, above all, on the fact that the Eucharist really is Jesus, under the appearances of bread and wine, and it is permitted only to those who believe this teaching.

St. Paul explains this:

> For I received from the Lord what I also delivered to you, that the Lord Jesus on the night when he was betrayed took bread, and when he had given thanks, he broke it, and said, "This is my body which is for you. Do this in remembrance of me."
>
> In the same way also the chalice, after supper, saying, "This chalice is the new covenant in my blood. Do this, as often as you drink it, in remembrance of me." For as often as you eat this bread and drink the chalice, you proclaim the Lord's death until he comes.
>
> *Whoever, therefore, eats the bread or drinks the cup of the Lord in an unworthy manner will be guilty of profaning the body and blood of the Lord. Let a man examine himself, and so eat of the bread and drink of the cup. For anyone who eats and drinks without discerning the body eats and drinks judgment upon himself.* That is why many of you are weak and ill, and some have died. (1 Corinthians 11:23–30; emphasis added)

This is the very heart of the matter. Notice that St. Paul warns against receiving the Eucharist "unworthily." By this he means being in the state of serious sin (1 John 5:16–17)—that is, "mortal sin," which extinguishes grace in the soul (see *CCC* 1855). Now, it isn't a stretch to assert that most people are quite prone to falling into serious sin, especially if they don't have the benefit of the sacraments to help keep them spiritually strong enough to resist temptations and, in the case of the sacrament of confession, to restore to the soul the life of grace when it is lost as a result of mortal sin.

What this means is that, all other things being equal, people who have never received the sacraments of the Eucharist and confession are not properly spiritually disposed to receive the Eucharist. They certainly can get to that point, by becoming Catholic and availing themselves of the sacraments, yes indeed, but before that happens, they're not properly prepared.

St. Paul makes a second key point here. Those people he describes who do not "discern," or recognize, the body (of Jesus) in the Eucharist are also told not to receive. Perhaps this is the situation your non-Catholic aunt is in when she attends a Catholic wedding. As a Baptist, she sincerely does not believe in the real presence of Christ in the Eucharist. While respectful of Catholic teaching on this point, she simply disagrees with and rejects it. This is a good example of not recognizing the Body.

And notice that in each instance—unworthiness (having fallen into serious sin) and not discerning the Body—St. Paul warns against receiving Communion. And the reasons he gives are alarming: They involve "profaning the body and blood of the Lord" and "eating and drinking judgment" upon oneself. Very dangerous!

This is why the Catholic Church does not allow non-Catholics to receive Holy Communion. It's not out of meanness or arrogance—far from it!—but out of a desire to protect people from doing something spiritually damaging ("That is why many of you are weak and ill, and some have died").

In this, the Church is like a lifeguard who calls out to someone about to jump into the deep end of the swimming pool, "If you don't know how to swim, don't jump in! It's dangerous!" Of course, once that person learns how to swim, he would be welcomed back and happily allowed to dive in. The Church does the same thing out of love and concern, lest anyone should, even if only inadvertently, cause himself any spiritual harm.

One final point: The Church's prohibition against receiving Holy Communion unworthily or without belief in the real presence applies just as fully to *Catholics*. This is why going to confession frequently is so important in the life of a committed Catholic. The graces you receive from the sacrament heal the self-inflicted wounds of sin and prepare you to receive the Lord in the Eucharist more worthily and fruitfully.

THE SEVEN SACRAMENTS IN THE BIBLE

The *Catechism* explains that "Christian initiation is accomplished by three sacraments together: Baptism which is the beginning of new life; Confirmation which is its strengthening; and the Eucharist which nourishes the disciple with Christ's Body and Blood for his transformation in Christ" (*CCC* 1275). These three, and most importantly baptism, are the foundations upon which all the other sacraments rest and have their stability and strength. We'll take a glance now at some of the prominent passages in which the seven sacraments appear in the pages of the Holy Bible, beginning with the foundational sacrament of baptism.

Baptism

This is *the* fundamental sacrament of the Catholic Church. Without it, one is unable to receive any of the other sacraments. Keep in mind that no one who is already Catholic can receive the sacrament of baptism, for that is what makes a person Catholic in the first place.

The Bible repeatedly shows us how important baptism is for beginning the Christian life, both because it is the doorway into the Church, the body of Christ, and because it regenerates the soul with the life-giving graces God pours into us when we receive it. Jesus commanded that "all nations" be baptized (see Matthew 28:19), and he reminds the apostles that baptism is necessary (see Mark 16:15 and John 3:3–5).

St. Paul calls baptism the "bath of regeneration" (see Ephesians 5:26) and "the washing of regeneration and renewal in the Holy Spirit" (see Titus 3:5), and St. Peter declares that when you are baptized, you gain "the forgiveness of your sins; and you shall receive the gift of the Holy Spirit" (Acts 2:38).[6]

The *Catechism* says that

> Baptism is birth into the new life in Christ. In accordance with the Lord's will, it is necessary for salvation, as is the Church herself, which we enter by baptism….
>
> The fruit of baptism, or baptismal grace, is a rich reality that includes forgiveness of original sin and all personal sins, birth into the new life by which man becomes an adoptive son of the Father, a member of Christ and a temple of the Holy Spirit. By this very fact the person baptized is incorporated into the Church, the body of Christ, and made a sharer in the priesthood of Christ.
>
> Baptism imprints on the soul an indelible spiritual sign, the character, which consecrates the baptized person for Christian worship. Because of the character baptism cannot be repeated. (*CCC* 1277, 1279–1280)

Confession (Penance)

We know from experience how easy it can be, when we stray from the protection of God's grace, to fall into sin. This tendency is due to concupiscence, which is the disordered inclination toward sin that we inherited, sadly, from our first parents, Adam and Eve. Don't feel as if you are alone in this struggle. Everyone shares it. As St. Paul himself says, we all must contend with this mysterious weakness when it comes to toppling into sin:

> I do not understand my own actions. For I do not do what I want, but I do the very thing I hate. Now if I do what I do not want, I agree that the law is good. So then it is no longer I that do it, but sin which dwells within me. For I know that nothing good dwells within me, that is, in my flesh. I can will what is right, but I cannot do it. For I do not do the good I want, but the evil I do not want is what I do. Now if I do what I do not want, it is no longer I that do it, but sin which dwells within me.
>
> So I find it to be a law that when I want to do right, evil lies close at hand. For I delight in the law of God, in my inmost self, but I see in my members another law at war with the law of my mind and making me captive to the law of sin which dwells in my members. Wretched man that I am! Who will deliver me from this body of death? Thanks be to God through Jesus Christ our Lord! So then, I of myself serve the law of God with my mind, but with my flesh I serve the law of sin. (Romans 7:15–25)

This is precisely why the Lord Jesus instituted the sacrament of confession: to help us extricate ourselves by God's grace when we've fallen into the pit of sin. The Bible abounds in warnings about the danger of sin and the need for repentance when we fall into sin (see Ezekiel 18:30, 33:11; Jeremiah 18:11, 25:5; Joel 2:12; Matthew 3:2, 4:7; Acts 2:38).

When Jesus "breathed on" his apostles and gave them the authority to forgive sins (see John 20:20–23), the sacrament of confession was born. Later, St. Paul described this apostolic "ministry of reconciliation" (2 Corinthians 5:18). Jesus also declared that the apostles had the authority to "bind and loose" their ministry on earth and in heaven (see Matthew 16:18, 18:18), and this authority goes hand in hand with his additional promise to them: "Whoever who listens to you listens to me" (Luke 10:16, *NAB*). Their successors, the bishops and priests, still carry out this authority by absolving us from our sins in the sacrament of confession, thus loosing us from the chains of iniquity.

See chapter 3 for more on confession and why you should make it a regular part of your spiritual life. It's the God-designed sacramental means for you to make a U-turn when, by your sins, you've deviated from the narrow path that leads to eternal life. Christian apologist C.S. Lewis explains why getting yourself back on track and heading back in the right direction (toward heaven) is so important:

> If you are on the wrong road, progress means doing an about turn and walking back to the right road; and in that case the man who turns back soonest is the most progressive man. We have all seen this when doing arithmetic. When I have started a sum the wrong way, the sooner I admit this and go back and start over again, the faster I shall get on. There is nothing progressive about being pigheaded and refusing to admit a mistake. And I think if you look at the present state of the world, it is pretty plain that humanity has been making some big mistake. We are on the wrong road. And if that is so, we must go back. Going back is the quickest way on.[7]

Jesus knows how often you and I need to stop, repent, turn around, get back on track, and head in the right direction again.[8]

The Holy Eucharist

In John 6:22–71 Jesus reveals most clearly the doctrine of his real presence in the Bread of Life, the Holy Eucharist. When he spoke of his followers eating his flesh and drinking his blood, his hearers understood him to be speaking literally (which he was), and even when many of them stopped following him because of this teaching, he did not call them back to say that they had misunderstood him. He didn't even hint that his teaching might be merely symbolic. And when those who fell away were gone, he turned to his apostles and asked if they too would depart.

Simon Peter's response is the perfect one for any Catholic, especially those who have difficulty grasping or hesitate to embrace this profound teaching: "Lord, to whom shall we go? You have the words of eternal life, and we have believed, and have come to know, that you are the Holy One of God" (John 6:68–69).

Jesus instituted the Sacrament of the Holy Eucharist at the Last Supper (see Matthew 26:26–28; Mark 14:22–34; Luke 22:15–20; 1 Corinthians 11:23–29). This was the first Mass ever celebrated, and it was here that Jesus ordained the apostles as priests, giving them the authority and power to confect the sacrament of the Eucharist when he told them, "Do this in memory of me." The Holy Sacrifice of the Mass was prophesied in Malachi 1:11: "For from the rising of the sun to its setting my name is great among the nations, and in every place incense is offered to my name, and a pure offering; for my name is great among the nations, says the Lord of hosts."[9]

There is deep and beautiful poetry in the Holy Eucharist that we can glimpse when we see how Christ's light illuminates previously obscure and mysterious things about the Old Covenant. The most ancient of these is the tree of the knowledge of good and evil in the Garden of

Eden (see Genesis 2:4–17; 3:1–7). See how, by eating the fruit of that tree, Adam and Eve committed the original sin and lost for themselves and for all human beings ever since (with one exception)[10] the many supernatural gifts God had originally intended for all human beings to have.

Christ "gave himself as nourishment," proclaimed Pope Urban IV (1195–1264),

> so that, since man had fallen through death, he might be lifted to life through food. Man fell by means of the food of the death-giving tree; man is raised up by means of the food of the life-giving tree. On the former hung the food of death, on the latter the nourishment of life. Eating the former earned a wound; the taste of this latter restored health. Eating wounded us, and eating healed us. See how the cure has come forth whence the wound arose, and life has come forth whence death entered in. Indeed, about that eating it was said, "On whatever day you eat it, you shall die' (Genesis 2:17); but about *this* eating, he [Jesus] has spoken: 'If anyone eats this bread, he shall live forever [John 6:51]."[11]

Other poetic biblical prefigurements and parallels with the Holy Eucharist include the ritual sacrifice of bread and wine offered by the mysterious king-priest Melchizedek (see Genesis 14:18–20), the Passover lamb (see Exodus 12; John 1:29, 19:36; 1 Corinthians 5:7), the manna in the desert, with which God fed the Israelites as they wandered in the desert before entering the Promised Land (see Exodus 16; John 6:31), the miraculous jar of flour a destitute widow used to bake bread for the Prophet Elijah, which strengthened him for his journey through the desert (see 1 Kings 17:1–17, 19:4–8), Christ's turning water into wine at the Wedding at Cana (see John 2:1–11), and his miraculous multiplications of loaves to feed the hungry multitudes (see Matthew 14:13–21; Mark 6:31–44; Luke 9:10–17; John 6:5–15).[12]

All of these biblical parallels help us understand more deeply how Jesus feeds, strengthens, and encourages us with his own Body and Blood in the Eucharist under the appearances of bread and wine.

Confirmation

Jesus promised that after he ascended to the Father, he would send the Church the "gift of the Holy Spirit" (see Luke 24:49; John 7:38, 14:16, 14:26, 16:7; Acts 1:5). Acts 2:4 tells of the first institution of the sacrament, when, in the form of tongues of flame, the Holy Spirit fell upon the apostles in the Upper Room. Since then, when a bishop anoints with oil and lays hands on a person being confirmed, the sacrament is conferred (see Acts 8:14–17), a glimpse of this being found in Acts 19:6 (cf. Hebrews 6:2). The *Catechism* says:

> Although confirmation is sometimes called the "sacrament of Christian maturity," we must not confuse adult faith with the adult age of natural growth, nor forget that the baptismal grace is a grace of free, unmerited election and does not need "ratification" to become effective. St. Thomas reminds us of this:
>
> > Age of body does not determine age of soul. Even in childhood man can attain spiritual maturity: as the Book of Wisdom says: "For old age is not honored for length of time, or measured by number of years." Many children, through the strength of the Holy Spirit they have received, have bravely fought for Christ even to the shedding of their blood. (*CCC* 1308)

A particularly striking biblical example of the power of the Holy Spirit in the sacrament of confirmation is found in the seventh chapter of the

Book of Acts, where we see St. Stephen, "full of the Holy Spirit" (Acts 7:55), courageously preach the truth of Jesus Christ to a hostile audience. His audience was so hostile, in fact, that Stephen's fearless proclamation of gospel enraged them to the point of stoning him to death, thus giving the Catholic Church its first martyr for the Faith. Countless more, strengthened by the grace of the Holy Spirit, have followed in Stephen's footsteps as they too ran the race toward heaven.

Holy Matrimony

The wedding between a man and a woman is symbolic of, and expresses in flesh and blood, the relationship between Christ and the Church (see Ephesians 5:31–32; Revelation 1:20, 17:7). Christ is the bridegroom, and the Church is the bride. Thus, the sacrament of holy matrimony enables the husband and wife to become a kind of icon of Christ and the Church (see Matthew 19:3; Ephesians 5:21–32).

Marriage is designed and ordained by God for two primary ends: The first is to perpetuate the human race through spouses' openness to life. This was God's original command to Adam and Eve, when he declared, "Be fertile and multiply" (Genesis 1:28, *NAB*; cf. Genesis 2:18–25). The second end of marriage is the mutual love and affection between husband and wife. This includes the freedom to express their love physically in the intimacy of romantic love and sexual intercourse.

God raised marriage in the order of grace from a natural covenant to a supernatural, sacramental covenant when the Lord was literally present at the marriage of his mother, the Blessed Virgin Mary, and his stepfather, St. Joseph (see Matthew 1:18–25; Luke 2:3–5). Later, at the wedding at Cana, Jesus performed his first miracle by turning water into wine (see John 2:1–11), further emphasizing his elevation of marriage to the level of a sacrament (see 1 Corinthians 7:2).

St. John Paul II spoke of this wondrous sacramental reality, saying:

This is what the Bible teaches in direct and eloquent language when it reports the joyful cry of the first woman, "the mother of all the living" (Genesis 3:20). Aware that God has intervened, Eve exclaims: "I have begotten a man with the help of the Lord" (Genesis 4:1). In procreation, therefore, through the communication of life from parents to child, God's own image and likeness is transmitted, thanks to the creation of the immortal soul. The beginning of the "book of the genealogy of Adam" expresses it in this way: "When God created man, he made him in the likeness of God. Male and female he created them, and he blessed them and called them man when they were created. When Adam had lived a hundred and thirty years, he became the father of a son in his own likeness, after his image, and named him Seth" (Genesis 5:1–3).

It is precisely in their role as co-workers with God who transmits his image to the new creature that we see the greatness of couples who are ready "to cooperate with the love of the Creator and the Savior, who through them will enlarge and enrich his own family day by day."… Thus, a man and woman joined in matrimony become partners in a divine undertaking: through the act of procreation, God's gift is accepted and a new life opens to the future.[13]

Holy Orders

In order to have a valid Eucharist, Mass must be celebrated. And in order to have the Mass, there must be validly ordained priests to celebrate it. This is the fundamental reason Jesus set apart certain men for the sacrificial service to the Church. We call them *priests*, which derives from the New Testament Greek word *presbuteros* (πρεσβύτερος), meaning "elder."

The three levels of holy orders are the diaconate, the priesthood, and the episcopacy. Deacons are ordained for service to the Church, especially (but not exclusively) in more mundane matters such as hospitality and feeding the poor, but also in preaching, teaching, administering baptism, and officially witnessing the sacrament of holy matrimony. Priests do all those things, as well as hear confessions, celebrate the Holy Sacrifice of the Mass, and anoint the sick (see the next section). Bishops, who have the fullness of the sacrament of holy orders, do all those things and also have the authority and power to ordain deacons and priests and to ordain priests to the episcopacy (see Acts 6:6, 14:22; 1 Timothy 4:14; 2 Timothy 5:22).

Jesus established the sacrament of holy orders at the Last Supper (see Matthew 26:26–29; Mark 14:22–34; Luke 22:15–20) by ordaining the apostles. This ordained ministry was extended to other approved men and has existed as a continual gift to the Church, the beginnings of which we see clearly mentioned in the Bible. St. Paul, for example, reminded Timothy, a young man who had been ordained and later consecrated as a bishop: "Do not neglect the gift you have, which was given you by prophetic utterance when the elders laid their hands upon you" (1 Timothy 4:14).

The Jewish Levitical priesthood of the Old Testament (see Hebrews 10:1–18) was only temporary; it could not actually accomplish the forgiveness of sins but rather, through ritual animal sacrifice and offerings in the temple, only symbolized it. However, the priesthood of the New Covenant, which Christ established, does have the power to do these things because it shares in Christ's own unique priesthood (see Hebrews 9:11–14, 23–28).

Anointing of the Sick (Extreme Unction, Holy Anointing)

When Jesus sent the apostles and the other disciples forth to cast out demons and heal the sick (see Mark 6:7–13), he commanded them to pray over people and to anoint them with oil. "So they went out and preached that men should repent. And they cast out many demons, and anointed with oil many that were sick and healed them" (Mark 6:12–13). In doing this, he had designated and empowered them to be "servants of Christ and stewards of the mysteries of God" (1 Corinthians 4:1).

The *Catechism* explains:

> Anointing with oil has all these meanings in the sacramental life. The pre-baptismal anointing with the oil of catechumens signifies cleansing and strengthening; the anointing of the sick expresses healing and comfort. The post-baptismal anointing with sacred chrism in Confirmation and ordination is the sign of consecration. By Confirmation Christians, that is, those who are anointed, share more completely in the mission of Jesus Christ and the fullness of the Holy Spirit with which he is filled, so that their lives may give off "the aroma of Christ." (*CCC* 1294)

St. James also gives us a clear description of the sacrament of anointing of the sick:

> Is any one among you suffering? Let him pray. Is any cheerful? Let him sing praise. Is any among you sick? Let him call for the elders of the church, and let them pray over him, anointing him with oil in the name of the Lord; and the prayer of faith will save the sick man, and the Lord will raise him up; and if he has committed sins, he will be forgiven. (James 5:13–15)

Today this sacrament, in which the priest anoints with oil a person who is seriously ill, may be accompanied by sacramental confession and the reception of Holy Communion.

CHAPTER THREE

FRIENDS OF DISTINCTION
Get to Know Our Lady and the Saints

JUST AS FOOD IS IMPORTANT TO HOLIDAY FAMILY GATHERINGS, EVEN more so is family itself. Try to imagine celebrating Christmas or Thanksgiving all by your lonesome. Not very appealing, is it?

We instinctively need and want the companionship of those we love, especially during those important milestones in life represented by holidays, holy days, and other events, such as baptisms, first Communions, weddings, and funerals. This natural human desire to share important occasions with family and friends is fulfilled in a far higher, more intimate, and superenhanced way in the glorious supernatural reality known as the communion of saints.

At the pinnacle of the assembly of human members of the body of Christ stands the mother of Jesus himself, the Blessed Virgin Mary, whom Catholics affectionately and reverently sometimes refer to as "Our Lady." This is not because of anything she did (or could do), but because of what God did for her by endowing her with special gifts of grace—from the moment of her conception—to enable her to live permanently free from all sin, including the condition of original sin (see Genesis 3:1–11; Romans 3:23, 5:19).

As St. John Paul II described her, the Blessed Virgin Mary is "the Church's own beginning" in that she was the first Christian—she was quite literally the very first person to whom the Good News of salvation in Jesus Christ was made known by the message of an angel (see Luke 1:26–35).[1] Mary was also the first Christian because, before anyone else, she said "yes" to God's plan of salvation in Jesus Christ by accepting his invitation to become the Mother of the Redeemer: "Behold, I am the handmaid of the Lord; let it be to me according to your word" (Luke 1:38).

Our Lady was also the first Christian in that, as soon as she said "yes" to the Good News and accepted Jesus Christ into her heart *and* her very body (through the virginal conception by the power of the Holy Spirit foretold by the Angel Gabriel), she immediately "went with haste" to tell others about Jesus (Luke 1:39–56).

Her complete and unhesitating *"Yes!"* to God's will was beautifully sublime and unreserved. Perhaps that's why St. John Paul II chose the Latin motto *Totus Tuus* ("Totally Yours") as his motto, in honor of Mary. For it was she who exemplified the total self-giving to God that all Christians are called to emulate.

Yes, the Catholic Church places a great deal of emphasis on the Blessed Virgin Mary, and rightly so. In addition to being the first Christian, she is also the one who not only contained within her own body the Incarnate Son of God for the nine months before the Virgin Birth, she also lived in the same home with Jesus Christ for the ensuing thirty years of his life until he launched out on his three-year public ministry.

Try to wrap your mind around what that means: Mary spent each day with Jesus Christ, one-on-one, for many of those years, not only being his beloved mother but learning from him as time passed.

Can you imagine a more personal relationship with Jesus (seeing him, hearing his voice, living with him for thirty years) than the one the Blessed Virgin Mary was blessed by the Triune God to experience? I certainly cannot imagine anything higher, more powerfully grace-filled, or Christ-centered than the life of Our Lady.

It is for these and related reasons that, as St. John Paul II said, she "'shines forth to the whole community of the elect as a model of the virtues.... 'Mary has already crossed the threshold between faith and that vision which is 'face to face'" (1 Corinthians 13:12).[2] This is why the Catholic Church places such an emphasis on Our Lady—though she is only a creature, she is nonetheless a holy example of Christian devotion to Jesus who we can all emulate.

Once you're a Catholic, you not only take up your own rightful place in the communion of saints as a member of the Church, you are also surrounded by a "great cloud of witnesses" (Hebrews 12:1), your brother and sister saints—on earth, in purgatory, and in heaven. There are three component parts of the body of Christ, all of which are united yet distinct:

1. The Church Triumphant: the blessed in heaven. They've made it! They've run the race and have received the crown of eternal life (see 2 Timothy 4:7) and are now with God in heaven, "perfected in righteousness" (see Hebrews 12:24). These are the ones who conquered sin and death by their patient endurance and fidelity to Christ (see Revelation 3:8–13).

2. The Church Suffering: the souls in purgatory. These have built their lives on the foundation of Christ but must yet undergo some purification of soul before entering into the beatific vision (i.e., seeing God face-to-face forever in heaven). In 1 Corinthians 3:10–15, St. Paul speaks about the period of purification these brothers and sisters in the body of Christ must undergo before entering into glory. Once they have finished their time of purification, they will enter into eternal life with God in heaven.

3. The Church Militant: those of us Catholics still in this mortal life. It is during our earthly life that, as St. Paul described it, we "fight

the good fight of the faith" (1 Timothy 6:12). This is why we call it the Church *militant*, for we are engaged in a battle for holiness against the world, the flesh, and the devil (see 1 John 2:16):

For though we live in the world we are not carrying on a worldly war, for the weapons of our warfare are not worldly but have divine power to destroy strongholds. We destroy arguments and every proud obstacle to the knowledge of God, and take every thought captive to obey Christ, being ready to punish every disobedience, when your obedience is complete.

Look at what is before your eyes. If anyone is confident that he is Christ's, let him remind himself that as he is Christ's, so are we. (2 Corinthians 10:3–7)

We face this struggle, by God's grace, with the weapons of the Spirit:

Finally, be strong in the Lord and in the strength of his might. Put on the whole armor of God, that you may be able to stand against the wiles of the devil. For we are not contending against flesh and blood, but against the principalities, against the powers, against the world rulers of this present darkness, against the spiritual hosts of wickedness in the heavenly places. Therefore take the whole armor of God, that you may be able to withstand in the evil day, and having done all, to stand. Stand therefore, having fastened the belt of truth around your waist, and having put on the breastplate of righteousness, and having shod your feet with the equipment of the gospel of peace; besides all these taking the shield of faith, with which you can quench all the flaming darts of the evil one. And take the helmet of salvation, and the sword of the Spirit, which is the word of God. (Ephesians 6:10–17)

An analogy that can help us understand these three distinct aspects of the Church—triumphant, suffering, and militant—is that of an army fighting its way back into its fort against an enemy army that besieges it. The head of the column has already entered into the fort; the second section lies wounded and in pain safely inside the gate but not completely within the fort; the third part, representing those of us in this earthly life, is still fighting its way into the fort, up the parapets, and across the drawbridge against the enemies who ring the outside of the fort and labor to prevent those soldiers from entering.

God's Family

Because the communion of saints encompasses all the members of the body of Christ—those on earth, those in purgatory, and those in heaven—it can be described most simply as God's family—that is, everyone who becomes his adopted sons and daughters through faith in Jesus Christ and sacramentally through baptism (see Romans 8:17, 8:29; Galatians 3:26; Titus 3:7).

At baptism, the Holy Spirit "pours out" God's grace into our hearts, regenerating us (this is the new birth in Christ) and transforming us into God's sons and daughters who now have a right relationship with him (i.e., we become justified) and, as a result, are intimately united to all the other members of God's family. We become one with Christ and with all who are in Christ. It's the ultimate family:

> But now in Christ Jesus you who once were far off have been brought near in the blood of Christ. For he is our peace, who has made us both one, and has broken down the dividing wall of hostility, by abolishing in his flesh the law of commandments and ordinances, that he might create in himself one new man in place of the two, so making peace, and might reconcile us

both to God in one body through the cross, thereby bringing the hostility to an end. And he came and preached peace to you who were far off and peace to those who were near; for through him we both have access in one Spirit to the Father. So then you are no longer strangers and sojourners, but you are fellow citizens with the saints and members of the household of God. (Ephesians 2:13–19)

The *Catechism* says that "the term 'communion of saints' has two closely linked meanings: communion in holy things (*sancta*) and [communion] among holy persons (*sancti*)" (*CCC* 948). This means that all the members of the mystical body of Christ share among themselves all the supernatural gifts with which Christ endows the Church, especially the Mass and the sacraments.

The Catholic Church is a rich and beautiful treasure-house of devotion to the Blessed Virgin Mary and the saints. The rosary, litanies, novenas, feast days, special prayers to saints, and so forth are intended to draw us closer to God by drawing us closer to his friends, those who love him most and best. The more like them we become, the more we glorify the Lord and become like him.

Archbishop Fulton Sheen was said to have compared the Catholic Church's focus on Mary and the saints to a young woman who, when the young man she loves asks her to marry him, expresses her great desire for him to meet her parents and siblings. How absurd it would be if the young man were to reply, "Wait. I love *you*. I'm not really interested in meeting your family." This strange reaction is the same as that of the Christian who says to Jesus, "I love you, Lord, but I have no interest in meeting and getting to know your mom or your friends."

The communion of saints is mentioned in the Apostles' Creed, one of the most ancient Christian statements of faith: "I believe in the Holy

Spirit, the holy Catholic Church, the communion of saints, the forgiveness of sins, the resurrection of the body, and the life everlasting. Amen."

The phrase "communion of saints" refers to the reality that all who are "in Christ" (see Romans 6:3-4, 8:1; Galatians 3:27) are also intimately united to each other in and through Christ. Just think of the Lord's teaching about the vine and the branches in John 15:5: "I am the vine, you are the branches. He who abides in me, and I in him, he it is that bears much fruit, for apart from me you can do nothing." Notice that each branch is connected to the vine, and therefore, each is also connected to all the other branches on the vine. It is in and through Jesus Christ that the branches enjoy a real unity with one another. And so it is with the members of his mystical body. Pope Pius XII described it this way:

> Our union in and with Christ is first evident from the fact that, since Christ wills His Christian community to be a Body which is a perfect Society, its members must be united because they all work together towards a single end....
>
> The more we become "members one of another" [Romans 12:5], "mutually careful, one for another" [1 Corinthians 12:25], the closer we shall be united with God and with Christ; as, on the other hand, the more ardent the love that binds us to God and to our divine Head, the closer we shall be united to each other in the bonds of charity.[3]

THE MYSTICAL BODY OF CHRIST

The analogy between a human body and the body of Christ, while apt and helpful, isn't an exact parallel. The body of Christ, Pope Pius XII explains, "is vastly superior to whatever bonds of union may be found in a physical or moral body."[4] Likewise, the members of the body of

Christ are nourished with supernatural food that is far more important and life-giving than the natural food we consume in this life to sustain our bodies.

This unity between all the members of the body of Christ comes about through the sacrament of baptism, when we are made members of the body of Christ, a motif St. Paul emphasized: "For just as the body is one and has many members, and all the members of the body, though many, are one body, so it is with Christ" (1 Corinthians 12:12; see also Romans 12:4–5). This is why the Catholic doctrine of the communion of saints is so integral to the Church's nature and mission in the world. It encompasses not only the spiritual interactions between members of the body of Christ who are still in this earthly life, but it crosses all boundaries of time and space, even death, to connect those here on earth with those in purgatory and in heaven.

There are four pillars of the doctrine of the communion of saints.

1. The Church is the body of Christ.

2. There is only one body of Christ, not one on earth and another in heaven.

3. Death does not separate the members of the body (see Romans 8:35–39).

4. Christians are bound by the law of Christ to love and pray for one another.

This is why St. Paul says:

> First of all, then, I urge that supplications, prayers, intercessions, and thanksgivings be made for all men, for kings and all who are in high positions, that we may lead a quiet and peaceable life, godly and respectful in every way. This is good, and it is acceptable in the sight of God our Savior, who desires all

men to be saved and to come to the knowledge of the truth. For there is one God, and there is one mediator between God and men, the man Christ Jesus. (1 Timothy 2:1–5)

Notice that it is because Christ is our one mediator with God that we are therefore able to "supplicate, pray, and intercede for others." And this, he says, is good and pleasing to God! Thus, you as a Catholic can ask the Blessed Virgin Mary and any other saints in heaven to pray for you, and because they are members of the one body of Christ and death does not separate us from each other, their prayers for you please God. There is no difference in kind between asking a fellow Catholic here on earth to pray for you and asking Mary to pray for you; there is only a difference in degree.

Since Christians are brought into God's family through Christ, and since they share in God's life-giving grace, they are united in a unique and powerful way. This allows us to love and care for one another, as we are commanded to do. The saints in heaven love and care for us, and so it is fitting that we pray to them and ask for their prayers, as we on earth assist one another through prayer.

A New Power of Holiness

The decision to become Catholic, or to return to the Catholic Church after a long absence, finds expression in the Lord's parable of the Prodigal Son (see Luke 15:11–32). This isn't to say that any given person necessarily lives the kind of debauched life of sin that Jesus attributes to the Prodigal Son (although many have, or still do). But the fact is, before receiving baptism, we are lost and astray, but once we are received into the Church, we are mightily transformed by God's grace. Consider St. Paul's vivid description of this transformation in Christ:

And you he made alive, when you were dead through the trespasses and sins in which you once walked, following the course of this world, following the prince of the power of the air, the spirit that is now at work in the sons of disobedience. Among these we all once lived in the passions of our flesh, following the desires of body and mind, and so we were by nature children of wrath, like the rest of mankind. But God, who is rich in mercy, out of the great love with which he loved us, even when we were dead through our trespasses, made us alive together with Christ (by grace you have been saved), and raised us up with him, and made us sit with him in the heavenly places in Christ Jesus, that in the coming ages he might show the immeasurable riches of his grace in kindness toward us in Christ Jesus (Ephesians 2:1–7).

This is reality of our newness in Christ is at the heart of the Catholic Church's answer to the age-old question, "Now what?" Now, we are to press forward in our relationship with the triune God. He enables us by his grace to do this through prayer, the sacraments, meditating on the Bible, good works of service to others, and saying "yes" to the constant opportunities for leading "a life worthy of the Lord, fully pleasing to him, bearing fruit in every good work and increasing in the knowledge of God" (Colossians 1:10).

Consider the related teaching given by the great fourth-century Church Father St. Cyril of Jerusalem:

This is in truth a serious matter, brethren, and you must approach it with good heed. Each one of you is about to be presented to God before tens of thousands of the Angelic Hosts: the Holy Ghost is about to seal your souls: you are to be enrolled in the army of the Great King. Therefore make you ready, and equip yourselves, by putting on, I mean, not bright apparel, but piety of soul with a good conscience. Regard not the Laver [i.e., baptism] as simple water, but rather regard the spiritual grace that is given with the water. For just as the offerings brought to the heathen altars, though simple in their nature, become defiled by the invocation of the idols, so contrariwise the simple water having received the invocation of the Holy Ghost, and of Christ, and of the Father, acquires a new power of holiness.[5]

Catholics must use this "new power of holiness" they have received from God. Those who fail to do so, never striving for the holiness of life and the love of God that the sacraments empower us to pursue, will languish in mediocrity and lukewarmness. (Let's not forget Jesus's harsh warning to those who are neither hot nor cold but who willfully remain lukewarm! See Revelation 3:15–18.) On the other hand, those who endeavor to correspond with God's graces are able to scale the heights of holiness. Just ask the saints.

To appreciate the Catholic approach to this subject, imagine that you are visiting a king. Entering his throne room, you hear beautiful music filling the air. Stepping into the chamber, you are dazzled: Gorgeous tapestries hang on the walls, stunning works of art adorn the room, and sumptuous carpet covers the floor. Attendants line the room, dressed in splendid clothing, their faces filled with happiness and their countenances shining with joy.

Moving into the room and approaching the king's throne, you notice that the room's grandeur intensifies. Reaching the foot of the throne, you look in awe upon the king. His magnificence is beyond description, more glorious than all the beauties you have seen or experienced. The royalty and beauty of his clothing, his crown, his scepter, and his throne overwhelm you. They are radiant, sparkling with precious gems and a mysterious light. Yet they are not the center of attention: The king is the focal point of all this glory. It is obvious that all of the room's beauty and light and magnificence are due to his person and his work; he has lavished his love and riches on everything and everyone around him.

Now, imagine you're visiting a different king in a different throne room. This throne room is unlike the first one in almost every way possible. There is no music; in fact, there is hardly any sound at all. Nothing catches your eye, for there is no artwork, no jewels, and no tapestries. There are no people! There is nothing at all, except for the king; there is nothing and no one to distract you from the king. He sits alone, in incredible glory on his regal throne at the far end of the long chamber. He is magnificent, yet his throne room is bare, silent, and strangely lacking.

Why is this second throne room this way, empty and cold and quiet? It is because this king is a jealous ruler who refuses to share his glory and riches and love. He wants no one to be distracted from him, and so he doesn't allow for even the smallest sounds, the tiniest of jewels, or even a single servant.

Both kings are glorious, impressive in so many ways. But the first king is more magnificent, for the sharing of his splendor and power and love is itself a glorious act of love. These two kings represent, of course, the different ways that Catholics and other Christians view God and his attitude toward creation, especially mankind.

The second king is analogous to how some perceive God and the saints. This king does not share his glory and wants no one and nothing else to receive attention, even for a few seconds. He is glorious, impressive, and powerful, but his drab and empty throne room is uninviting and hollow.

The first king represents the Catholic (and Eastern Orthodox) understanding of God and how he treats his friends, the saints. His glory knows no bounds, and he lavishes it on those who surround him—they are his family! And we know that those who behold "the glory of the Lord, are being transformed into the same image from glory to glory, just as from the Lord, the Spirit" (2 Corinthians 3:18).

God is not worried that you'll look at the beautiful tapestries or the sparkling jewels or the perfect clothing of the others in the throne room. Those are all part of his glory, and marveling at them brings more honor and glory to God the King. The splendor suffusing all that surrounds him is evidence of his glory—without his glory there would not be music and jewels and beautiful clothing. All of those things lead us to him, who creates them and makes them what they are. They cause us to focus on him as the source of all glory.

The saints share in God's glory, for they are God's new creation through Jesus Christ. St. Paul explains, "Therefore if any one is in Christ, he is a new creation; the old has passed away, behold, the new has come" (2 Corinthians 5:17). This new creation radiates God's glory, for God fills the saints with his grace. He shares his glory, his divine life, with those who are willing to receive it through the work and person of Jesus Christ.

You Have Friends in High Places

Another central aspect of the communion of saints is the role that the Blessed Virgin Mary and the rest of the holy men and women of the Church triumphant play in the life of the body of Christ, namely, as intercessors for us before the throne of God in heaven.

But, some ask, how can they be mediators when the Bible declares: "There is one God and there is one mediator between God and men, the man Christ Jesus" (1 Timothy 2:5)? It might appear at first glance that by asking for the intercession of saints, Catholics are in conflict with this biblical teaching. Worse yet, some non-Catholics argue that honoring the Blessed Virgin Mary and the saints in heaven and asking them to pray for us is tantamount to worshipping them. This is a serious misunderstanding of the actual Catholic teaching, and it needs to be clarified.

First, because all Christians are members of the body of Christ, they take part in a communion of faith, experiencing fellowship, partaking in the sacraments and the liturgies and all of the spiritual graces and goods that flow from Christ's Church. The Church is the Father's goal for humanity and is animated by the Holy Spirit; those who enter into Christ's body do so by being baptized in the "name of the Father, and of the Son, and of the Holy Spirit." In other words, we enter into the Trinitarian life and are filled with God's grace, his supernatural life.

Therefore, all Christians participate and enjoy a vital communion, a dynamic organic unity with Christ and with every other member of His body, and it is not limited to Christians here on earth, but transcends time and space, for it is supernatural. This unity, which cannot exist apart from God's grace, the work of his Son, and the presence of the Holy Spirit, is the core of the doctrine of the communion of saints. Pope Paul VI explained:

> There reigns among men, by the hidden and benign mystery of the divine will, a supernatural solidarity whereby the sin of one harms the others just as the holiness of one also benefits the others. Thus the Christian faithful give each other mutual aid to attain their supernatural aim. A testimony of this solidarity is manifested in Adam himself, whose sin is passed on through propagation to all men. But of this supernatural solidarity the greatest and most perfect principle, foundation and

example is Christ himself to communion with Whom God has called us.

Indeed Christ "committed no sin," "suffered for us," was wounded for our iniquities, bruised for our sins...by his bruises we are healed."

Following in the footsteps of Christ, the Christian faithful have always endeavored to help one another on the path leading to the heavenly Father through prayer, the exchange of spiritual goods and penitential expiation. The more they have been immersed in the fervor of charity, the more they have imitated Christ in his sufferings, carrying their crosses in expiation for their own sins and those of others, certain that they could help their brothers to obtain salvation from God the Father of mercies. This is the very ancient dogma of the Communion of the Saints, whereby the life of each individual son of God in Christ and through Christ is joined by a wonderful link to the life of all his other Christian brothers in the supernatural unity of the Mystical Body of Christ till, as it were, a single mystical person is formed....

Therefore the union of the wayfarers with the brethren who have gone to sleep in the peace of Christ is not in the least weakened or interrupted, but on the contrary, according to the perpetual faith of the Church, is strengthened by a communication of spiritual goods. For by reason of the fact that those in heaven are more closely united with Christ, they establish the whole Church more firmly in holiness, lend nobility to the worship which the Church offers to God here on earth and in many ways contribute to building it up evermore (1 Corinthians 12:12–27). For after they have been received into their heavenly home and are present to the Lord (2 Corinthians 5:8), through him and with him and in him they do not cease to intervene with the Father for us, showing forth the merits which they have won on earth through the one Mediator between God and man, Jesus Christ (1 Timothy 2:5), by serving God in all things and filling up in their flesh those things which are lacking of the sufferings of Christ for his Body which is the Church (Colossians 1:24). Thus by their brotherly interest our weakness is greatly strengthened.[6]

Note the pope's repeated references to the "supernatural" reality of the unity Christians share. Because of the sacrificial life and love of Jesus Christ, Christians participate in his inheritance and become by grace what he is by nature: a child of God.

As we saw earlier, this is repeatedly taught in the New Testament. The doctrine of the communion of saints is not just an isolated belief, but permeates all of Catholic teaching. If we fail to appreciate what the communion of saints is, we will misunderstand, or not comprehend well enough, the nature and mission of the Church, the meaning and power of the liturgy and the sacraments, God's salvific plan for humanity, even the life, death, and resurrection of Jesus Christ himself. All of these realities depend, in small ways and large, on that single tenet in the Apostles' Creed: "I believe in the communion of saints."

The reality of this communion is beyond our total comprehension, yes, but we must work to understand it better, for it affects so many aspects of our lives—even though we often don't realize it! Moreover, while it helps us now, in our daily lives, it extends far beyond our fleeting, earthly fellowship. It is a communion, a sharing, of spiritual goods, involving intercession, prayers, and the often misunderstood practices of honoring and venerating God's friends, the saints.

Going back to the analogy of the two kings: Here on earth, we venerate our brothers and sisters who have gone before us to heaven, precisely because the Lord, by welcoming them into heaven, has showered them with unbelievable glory and honor and praise. As Father, he welcomes home his children, just as the father of the Prodigal Son embraced his wayward son when he returned home. And so the communion of saints is our joining in this heavenly celebration, a participation in the honor given by God to the saints.

This Means You!

As a Catholic, your mission is to tell others the truth about what the Catholic Church teaches—for example, about the Blessed Virgin Mary and the saints. When you find yourself wondering, "Now what?" after your entrance into the Catholic Church, here's a great answer: Tell others about the role of Our Lady and the saints in the life of the Church and why they are very important to all Christians.

Notice that quite a few non-Catholics have difficulties with this issue. They might agree that there is a unity among believers, but they do not agree on the nature and means of that unity. They agree that it is brought about by the Holy Spirit, but they say that Christians are not actually filled with God's divine life, which we call grace (i.e., God infusing or pouring out his grace into our souls).

Some non-Catholics think that the unity of Christians is based on shared external beliefs about the Bible and Jesus Christ, not on a recognition of the inner transformation wrought by the Holy Spirit. Many have a hard time conceiving of a unity that involves people who have left this earth long ago. Therefore, they cannot admit the logical implications the Catholic Church draws, which are, as we have seen:

- Our unity in and through Christ transcends time and space;
- Our unity involves all Christians, whether in heaven, on earth, or in purgatory;

- Our unity carries a natural—or supernatural--obligation of charity and mutual support.

The foundation of this doctrine is that God is one, that he alone is holy, and that he alone deserves worship and adoration. Again and again the ancient Hebrew people were reminded of these essential truths: "Hear, O Israel! The Lord our God is one Lord, and you shall love the Lord your God with all your heart and with all your soul and with all your might" (Deuteronomy 6:4–5; see also Deuteronomy 6:13–14). Repeatedly they failed to heed these words, falling into idolatry and the worship of false gods. And continually, the Bible tells us, they wandered away from God and followed false teachings and pagan practices.

There are many today who accuse Catholics of these same failures. Some Protestants claim, often in strident and harsh tones, that the Catholic Church is Christian in name only—that Catholics, by honoring the saints and praying to them, fall into idolatry and pagan practices. *God alone* must be the recipient of our praise and prayers, they insist; otherwise we take what rightly belongs to the Creator and give it to mere mortal creatures. Devotional practices that involve honoring Mary and the saints, praying to them, and asking for their aid are often attacked with strong rhetoric.

Such criticisms demand a response, not only because there are solid Catholic answers to these objections, but also because there are serious problems with the attitudes and assumptions behind them. By addressing these claims, Catholics can better understand the importance of the communion of saints and more deeply appreciate that we truly do have friends in high places.

As we will see, many of the perceived problems with the Catholic belief in the communion of saints are just that: matters of perception. The Catholic Church has always taught that God alone deserves worship, that he alone is to be adored, and that he alone saves us from our sins. It is a sin to worship any creature (i.e., the sin of idolatry). It doesn't logically follow, however, that honoring those who are united to God and who are holy in his sight—the saints—takes anything away from God. Because the saints, those on earth and those in heaven, are children of God and our brothers and sisters in Christ, they are our dearest friends. And the bond of friendship that we share is the grace, the supernatural life, that God has given us through his Son, Jesus Christ, and in the power of the Holy Spirit.

Put another way, we cannot honor our brothers and sisters, the saints, any more than God has already honored them by making them his children. After all, it was Jesus himself who declared to the Father, "*The glory which you have given me I have given to them,* that they may be one even as we are one" (John 17:22).

St. John writes, "See what love the Father has given us, that we should be called children of God; and such we are. The reason why the world does not know us is that it did not know him" (1 John 3:1). This points to another important aspect of Catholic teaching on Mary and the saints: grace and what it does to the soul.

PARTAKERS OF THE DIVINE NATURE

The Catholic Church emphasizes that we are saved by grace alone: "For by grace you have been saved through faith; and this is not your own doing, it is the gift of God" (Ephesians 2:8). This divine gift is really a share in God's own inner life (think of the sap in the vine, which animates all the branches, or the blood in the body, which animates all the members of the body). It is as if, by bestowing his grace on us in the sacraments, God gives us a divine blood transfusion, his eternal life being poured into our souls, enabling and preparing us to be united with him—to become like him—so we can be ready to live with him in heaven for all eternity.

Because the saints in heaven, the Church triumphant, are "partakers of the divine nature" in the fullest possible measure (2 Peter 1:4), they experience complete communion with God because they have been fully transformed by his grace.

The souls in purgatory are in the final phase of that transformation, and as soon as it is complete and the effects of their sins in this life have been fully expiated (i.e., "burned away"; see 1 Corinthians 3:10ff), they will immediately enter into eternal life and the beatific vision.

And we in the Church militant who are still, as St. Paul says, working out our "salvation in fear and trembling" (see Philippians 2:12) and "fighting the good fight" (see 1 Timothy 6:12 and 2 Timothy 4:7) should seek to cooperate with God's grace so that when the end of this mortal life comes, we will be found "blameless and innocent" (see Philippians 2:15) and ready to be with the Lord in heaven.

That's the ultimate, final meaning of "communion" in the doctrine of the communion of saints. It's not mere togetherness or camaraderie, but a true, lasting, and profound unity with all the members of the body and branches on the vine because of our union with Christ.

It is a communion primarily and most importantly with God himself. And it extends to every single member of God's family, the one body of Christ, the Church: "For just as we have many members in one body and all the members do not have the same function, so we, who are many, are one body in Christ, and individually members one of another" (Romans 12:4–5). This is why we on earth in the Church militant ask for the intercessory prayers of those saints in heaven—just as we ask for prayer from Christians here on earth--and their intercession on our behalf is "good and pleasing to God our savior" (1 Timothy 2:3, *NAB*).

Likewise, we venerate the relics of those saints in glory and their sacred images because they remind us of these real men and women who loved God, who fought the good fight, and who now reign with the Blessed Trinity as priests and kings forever. Mary and the saints are our models in faith. They are the brothers and sisters who teach us how to love and follow and obey Christ.

The great German theologian Karl Adam observes, "The Catholic cannot think of the good God without thinking at the same time of the Word made Flesh, and of all His members who are united to Him by faith and love in a real unity."[7] This real unity is biblical and it is the basis for the Catholic model of the communion of saints. Because we love God, we are filled with his life, and we love His friends. And we know that because God loves us, his friends love us, too: "Beloved, let us love one another; for love is from God, and [everyone] who loves is born of God and knows God" (1 John 4:7).

How the Saints Hear Our Prayers

Even so, you might be asking yourself how it is possible for the Blessed Virgin Mary and the rest of the saints, our fellow, finite human beings, to simultaneously hear all of the many prayers directly toward them? Wouldn't this require them to be all-knowing and all-powerful, just like God? Isn't this ascribing to Mary and the saints attributes that belong only to the Almighty Creator?

We must keep in mind that life in heaven is quite different from life on earth. Heaven is not bound by space and time, and those who dwell there do not experience the same temporal limitations as we do. To wonder how long it would take a saint to hear a hundred prayers, or a thousand, or a billion, is to overlook the fact that time is not an issue for the saints in heaven. They are not all-knowing or all-powerful, but they don't need to be in order to hear our supplications for their prayers of intercession. They are living in a different dimension, utterly unfettered by earthly boundaries.

One way to understand this truth more clearly is to imagine the difference between life in the womb and the life we all experience once we're born. If you could somehow communicate with an unborn child and try to explain to her what life will be like outside the womb, she wouldn't be able to comprehend it. How could you possibly explain chocolate chip cookies, the ocean, thunderstorms, music, dancing, romance, honesty, truth, algebra, the moon, the color blue, picnics, fireworks, and the Milky Way to an unborn child?

It's impossible. Not because those things aren't real, obviously, but because a child in the womb has no capacity to understand them and how much *more* life will become when she is born. And even if she could understand the concepts, nothing in her dark, small, prebirth existence within her mother's womb could possibly prepare her to imagine all that awaits her in the life to come outside the womb. Something similar is at work for us as we try, in vain, to imagine how the saints live and love and what unthinkably amazing things they are enabled by God's grace to do. As St. Paul said, *"What no eye has seen, not ear heard, nor the heart of man conceived, what God has prepared for those who love him"* (1 Corinthians 2:9).

This is why, when you consider the question logically, even though perhaps you cannot imagine how a saint can hear and understand all those prayers, you can see there is no reason why a saint cannot do this, because the number of prayers ascending to heaven, no matter how great, is still finite. There could never be an infinite number of prayers. Therefore, neither omniscience (infinite all-knowing) nor omnipresence (infinite presence everywhere at all times) is required in order for all prayers to be heard.

The saints in heaven have abilities that we cannot fathom, for they are freed from the corruption of sin and, now beyond time and space, are no longer limited by them. Living in heaven is to be with Christ and to share fully in his life. This doesn't mean that the saints are deities, but they are *deified*—that is, they are full sharers in the divine nature (see 2 Peter 1:4). They have been transformed into the image of Christ's glorified and resurrected body. Free from sin and full of God's life, they are capable of things we can barely begin to imagine. As St. John writes, "We are God's children now; it does not yet appear what we shall be, but we know that when he appears we shall be like him, for we shall see him as he is" (1 John 3:2).

After his resurrection, Jesus astounded his disciples by walking through walls and disappearing in the light of day (see John 20:19). A similar glorified body has been promised to those who are God's friends, the saints. "We shall be like him," St. Paul states (see Philippians 3:20–21). We cannot pretend to understand how this is or what it will be like, but we cannot deny that the saints in heaven share in unimaginable glory: "What no eye has seen, nor ear heard, / nor the heart of man conceived, / what God has prepared for those who love him" (1 Corinthians 2:9).

Now, it's true that God alone "knows the hearts of all the children of men" (1 Kings 8:39; 2 Chronicles 6:30). God says, "I the Lord search the mind / and test the heart" (Jeremiah 17:10; see also Romans 8:27), and "I am the searcher of hearts and minds" (Revelation 2:23, *NAB*). Yes, it's true that only God is all-knowing. But this does not mean that humans cannot know anything. In fact, when God allows it, we human beings can know a great deal about what's in another person's mind. Take, for example, the case of St. Peter, who was able to know the private thoughts of Ananias and Sapphira, who had lied to him (see Acts 5:1–11).

Recognizing that the saints have a supernatural kind of knowledge, permitted them by God, does not mean that they have knowledge to the same degree as God. They cannot know infinitely or perfectly, but they can know, just as all humans can know many things. So while it is true that I cannot know to the degree that God does, I can know, even if imperfectly. Created in the image of God, men and women, by God's grace, have free will, an intellect, and knowledge.

Now, in order for the saints to hear our prayers, we must ask for their prayers! Catholics do not believe that the saints are able to look inside our minds and read our thoughts without our consent. Those who say they do misrepresent Catholic teaching. It isn't a matter of mind reading, but of asking and hearing.

The intercession of the saints relies on our communicating our requests to the saints, just as we communicate our needs and requests to our friends and fellow Christians here on earth. And when we make those requests to those around us, we reveal our private thoughts and inner intentions, as human discourse requires. In fact, human communication is an attribute given by God and one that reflects the communication between the Persons of the Trinity, and the communication of His Word—both written and spoken—to humanity.

The Catholic Church has always clearly taught that Mary and the saints are mere mortal creatures. They are honored by God and cherished in heaven, but they are still creatures and always will be. Created in the image of God, man does have "a unique place in creation" (*CCC* 355) but always as a creature. No amount of holiness or closeness to God can change this fact—and Catholics do not argue otherwise.

There is clear biblical evidence that God, by his power and grace, allows the saints in heaven to know of the actions and thoughts of people on earth. We know that those in heaven, both angels and saints, know of and rejoice over each sinner who repents:

> I tell you, in just the same way there will be more joy in heaven
> over one sinner who repents than over ninety-nine righteous

people who have no need of repentance.... I tell you, there will be rejoicing among the angels of God over one sinner who repents." (Luke 15:7, 10, *NAB*)

We do not know, of course, how they are aware of these individual decisions and actions, but just because we don't understand the mysteries of heaven doesn't mean they are fabrications. After all, the Lord promised that his friends in heaven would possess great and glorious abilities. "So also is the resurrection of the dead. [The body] is sown corruptible; it is raised incorruptible," writes Paul. "It is sown dishonorable; it is raised glorious. It is sown weak; it is raised powerful" (1 Corinthians 15:42–43, *NAB*).

Heaven, according to the *Catechism*, "is the blessed community of all who are perfectly incorporated into Christ" (*CCC* 1026). That is why heaven is an amazing place filled with people capable of doing amazing things. It is by God's grace, and it is beyond our comprehension. Man is not made God, but by being in full communion with God, he shares in the glorious riches of the King and shares those riches with the saints on earth.

CHAPTER FOUR

Smells and Bells

Become Familiar with Catholic Piety, Calendars, Customs, and Quirks

Compare the way you look in your baby pictures with how you look today. Big difference, right? You look nothing like you did then, but that's to be expected because your body has grown, matured, and taken on new characteristics that you didn't have when you were a year old. The same is true of the Church, the body of Christ. It, too, has undergone a continual, two thousand–year metamorphosis from infancy to the mature form we know today. And that is to be expected, for the Church is a living organism, and like your body, it grows and develops and changes in appearance, without ever ceasing to be the same Church that Christ established.

Jesus predicted this would happen when he told the parable of the mustard seed:

> With what can we compare the kingdom of God, or what parable shall we use for it? It is like a grain of mustard seed, which, when sown upon the ground, is the smallest of all the seeds on earth; yet when it is sown it grows up and becomes the greatest of all shrubs, and puts forth large branches, so that the birds of the air can make nests in its shade. (Mark 4:30–32)

The infant Church we glimpse in the four Gospels and in the Acts of the Apostles looks quite different from its present state, just as the tiny mustard seed differs greatly from the large tree it will eventually become. But the tree is the same entity as the seed, and the Church today is the same one you read about in the New Testament. The externals have changed and developed, but the identity remains identical. So it should not surprise you to see the Church depicted in such primitive terms in the New Testament, without all the precise theolog- . ical vocabulary and detailed liturgies that would develop over time. To be astonished by such natural growth would be as unreasonable as to expect an adult woman to look the same as she did when she was baby.

Over the past two thousand years of Catholic history, a vast and beautiful heritage of rituals, practices, and conventions has developed in the Church, not haphazardly or randomly, but as the result of an organic growth in response to needs and desires of God's people; for example, the need to express precisely what the Bible teaches about Mary (e.g., the Church calls her the Mother of God) or the desire to celebrate key moments in the life of Our Lord (e.g., the Church celebrates the feasts of Christmas and Easter).

An analogy for this change is the way highways developed in the United States. Before the advent of the automobile, roads tended to be narrow and unpaved and did not require signal lights, safety signs, and lane stripes, which the traffic—horses, carts, and carriages—managed without. But once cars came on the scene, roads evolved. Little by little, signs, paved surfaces, and other improvements were added as a natural development of the highway system, to meet the needs of the time. Theoretically, if the promise of flying cars is ever realized, lane strips, on-ramps, and guard rails will go the way of the dodo because they will no longer be needed.

The Catholic Church has likewise developed, but with a difference. The vast majority of the customs that have developed over time remain to this day and will continue, one can assume, until Jesus returns at the end of the world, because, unlike roads, which change with technology, human nature does not change, nor should those practices and benign human traditions that grew up naturally in the Church to meet its needs and to enable us to worship God and serve one another more fully.

A perfect example of this is the Holy Bible. The apostles did not have a Bible with an Old and New Testament compiled into a single volume as you and I have today. It would take centuries. First the New Testament would be have to be written and then the Old and New Testaments would be combined. But what a great development it is, and how fortunate we are to have the Bible, something that will never go out of style or become obsolete before Christ returns.

It is these important and beneficial external characteristics of the Catholic Church that we will consider now, keeping in mind that these later developments in prayer, liturgy, spirituality, canon law, and so forth are good and helpful and reflect order and cohesion among the members of the body of Christ.

New Catholics who ask themselves with a shrug, "Now what do I do?" will find that it helps to get a handle on the finer details of key Catholic realities in the area of spirituality, good works, and liturgy. Understanding these things more deeply will really help you enter into your lifelong calling to live out the Catholic faith in your daily life.

PRAYER

A major legacy of the Catholic Church's two thousand–year treasury of wisdom is its immense reservoir of prayers and devotions. Just think

of all the profound meditations and insights that your Catholic fore-
fathers have bequeathed to you in their rich and beautiful prayers of
praise, thanksgiving, and petition. Don't neglect them. By all means,
learn them and assimilate them into your heart and mind, letting them
breathe into your soul the richness of the truths of the faith and a desire
for union with God.

These prayers are like a magnificent paving stones on that narrow
path that leads to eternal life (see Matthew 7:13), engraved with beautiful, inspirational images and lessons about the truths of the Faith. As
you move onward and upward along this blessed path, you will learn
and mature as a Christian to the extent that you pay attention and make
those truths part of you, realizing that they are leading you toward
heaven:

> Enter by the narrow gate; for the gate is wide and the way is
> easy, that leads to destruction, and those who enter by it are
> many. For the gate is narrow and the way is hard, that leads to
> life, and those who find it are few. (Matthew 7:13–14)

The Church's liturgical prayers include those of the Mass (such as the
Our Father, the Gloria, and the Creed) and of the Divine Office (such as
the Magnificat and the Benedictus). Non-liturgical prayers include the
holy Rosary, the Angelus, and various novenas (prayers that are offered
for a fixed number of days, usually nine), to name a few.

EUCHARISTIC ADORATION

When Jesus entered the Garden of Gethsemane on the night he was
betrayed, he beckoned his three closest associates, the apostles Peter,
James, and John, to stay and pray with him.

> "My soul is very sorrowful, even to death; remain here, and
> watch with me." And going a little farther he fell on his face

and prayed, "My Father, if it be possible, let this chalice pass from me; nevertheless, not as I will, but as you will." And he came to the disciples and found them sleeping; and he said to Peter, "So, could you not watch with me one hour? Watch and pray that you may not enter into temptation; the spirit indeed is willing, but the flesh is weak." (Matthew 26:38–40)

This Bible passage reveals why Eucharistic Adoration is so important in the Catholic Church. By spending time with Jesus in Eucharistic Adoration, you can respond to his invitation to watch one hour with him. (This is why it is customary for Catholics to commit to a regular weekly hour of adoration, but the Church encourages every Catholic to make some time, even if just a few minutes, for the devotion.) It's a chance for you to spend some quiet time with Jesus, adoring and praising him, thanking him, and also sharing with him your heart's desires, fears, hopes, and needs.

What could possibly be better, this side of eternity, than being present before the Lord in intimate conversation like that? I know a woman who takes time during adoration to write reflections in her journal as a way to meditate on how God is working in her life and to get her spiritual batteries recharged in the process.

Consider the disciples who encountered the risen Jesus on the road to Emmaus (see Luke 24:13–35). They didn't even recognize him, yet, listening to him explain the Scriptures had filled them with such joy that when they reached their destination, they begged him, "Stay with us, for it is toward evening and the day is now far spent" (Luke 24:29).

You will do well to realize that in this fleeting life, it is already well toward evening and the day is far spent. What better way is there, outside of the Mass itself, for Jesus to stay with you, as he did with those disciples, than by visiting him in Eucharistic Adoration?

When you find yourself asking, "Now what?" as a new Catholic, make Eucharistic Adoration part of your faith life. You'll be amazed and grateful to Our Lord when you see how it calms, focuses, and grounds you in his loving embrace.

PIETY

The word *piety* might conjure up images of little old ladies silently praying during Mass while clasping rosary beads in gnarled fingers, or penitential pilgrims at the Shrine of Our Lady of Guadalupe in Mexico walking on their knees as a mortification. If that's what you picture when you think of piety, that's good, because these things are part of Catholic piety, albeit a small part. But there is vastly more involved.

Webster's dictionary defines piety as "devotion to God" or "dutifulness in religion." This is an apt description of what it means in the Catholic Church, though it is also a very good example of Catholic pluriformity in unity.

There is no single, monolithic version of Catholic piety. Rather, we can say, there is a Spirit-filled energy of piety in the Catholic Church, a spiritual élan or impetus within the body of Christ that animates Catholics (at least those who are plugged in and paying attention) to live out their love for Jesus, Mary, the saints, and their fellow man through external acts of service, devotion, and spirituality.

Reading the Bible is a very important form of Catholic piety. Spending time immersed in and attentive to God's written Word will help you cultivate virtue and root out vice, learn how to deal justly and charitably with your neighbor and to face fear and failures, temptations and troubles.

Other excellent forms of Catholic piety include attending daily Mass, praying the Rosary, wearing the Miraculous Medal, lighting votive candles, spending time in eucharistic adoration, reverently making the sign of the cross, praying for the souls in purgatory, working at a soup kitchen, volunteering at a pregnancy support center, visiting prisoners, and praying the Stations of the Cross (in which we meditate on fourteen key biblical episodes in Christ's passion and crucifixion). These and many other forms of piety are integral to the Catholic life, and the best part is that you are free to gravitate to whichever ones you find most edifying and helpful to you as you grown in your knowledge of and love for Christ and his Church. These various acts of piety are like multivitamins for your soul: they are meant to help strengthen your connection to the Lord and his people through praying, doing, reading, and sharing.

Don't be put off by the word piety. It is not a synonym for *stuffy*, *old-fashioned*, or *pre-Vatican II*. It is, rather, a way of being Catholic in real, tangible, and spiritually beneficial ways. Or think of it this way: Piety is to being happily Catholic as giving your wife a dozen roses on your anniversary is to being happily married. It always helps!

Confession

The sacrament of confession, also known as reconciliation or penance, plays a very important—really, indispensable—role in the lives of devout Catholics. In this great sacrament, we encounter Jesus the way the leper did in Mark 1:40–42. He approached the Lord and begged, "If you will, you can make me clean." And Jesus, having pity on the man, "stretched out his hand and touched him, and said to him, 'I will; be clean.' And immediately the leprosy left him, and he was made clean."

You and I, as guilty sinners, are like the leper who asks for healing. In the sacrament of confession, the Lord does heal us, for, as the Bible teaches, "If we confess our sins, he is faithful and just, and will forgive our sins and cleanse us from all unrighteousness" (1 John 1:9). Sin, like leprosy, is disfiguring and harmful to others.

Notice, though, that the Lord doesn't just heal the leper and then dismiss him. He tells him, "Go, show yourself to the priest, and offer for your cleansing what Moses commanded, for a proof to the people" (Mark 1:44). This corresponds exactly with the sacrament of confession because our sins are not just between us and God. They damage our relationship with the entire body of Christ (see 1 Corinthians 12:26), and that relationship must be repaired. When Jesus breathed on the apostles and gave them power and authority to forgive sins (see John 20:19–23), he commissioned them to do spiritually for sinners what he had done physically for the leper.

This is why living the Catholic faith well involves going to confession frequently—which, for most laypeople translates to, say, once a month. You're certainly free to go to confession as frequently as necessary (that's why Jesus instituted this sacrament, after all—to help us get out of the ditch when we run ourselves off the road to eternal life by committing serious sin), but you should strive to go regularly and at the very least, once a year.

Smells and Bells

British playwright William Congreve wrote, "Music has charms to sooth a savage breast, to soften rocks, or bend a knotted oak."[1] If music alone, appealing to the sense of hearing, can achieve such effects, it is no wonder that the Catholic Church, in its liturgy and its sacraments, engages the whole person, body and soul, mind and senses.

The Catholic Church has a long and venerable tradition of employing beautiful things to energize our minds and lift our spirits heavenward toward God and heavenly realities. These include incense, candles—including the red votive lamp in the sanctuary (usually a candle surrounded by red glass that gives off a scarlet glow) as a reminder that Christ is present in the tabernacle—holy water, medals, bells that ring from the bell tower, and bells that ring at Mass when the altar server announces the Consecration. Our bodily senses of sight, smell, and hearing are enriched and our minds more ordered toward God through these physical displays of beauty. These smells and bells, of course, are not themselves the focus, but are aides. They are like a paved road that makes it easier for a car to move forward toward its destination, or a gust of wind that fills the sails of our minds and helps us move onward toward home port.

SACRED VESSELS

Catholic priests use sacred vessels to accomplish their God-given mission of saving souls by being the primary dispensers of the Holy Mysteries we call the sacraments. The sacred vessels used at the altar during Mass and special devotions are these:

- Ciborium: This large cup or bowl, lined with gold, holds hosts to be consecrated by a priest during Mass for Holy Communion or consecrated hosts to be reserved in the tabernacle. At the Consecration, what are merely wafers of unleavened bread become the Body and Blood, soul and divinity of the risen Lord Jesus Christ, and the Church from time immemorial has used the ciborium as a suitable container in which to store them, whether before or after they are consecrated. The tight-fitting lid helps preserve freshness, prevents contamination from insects or dust, and serves as a noble vessel for the Lord's Body in the Holy Eucharist.

- Chalice: This traditionally solid-metal ornate cup, often gold- or silver-plated, or at least having a gold finish,[2] holds wine that will become the precious Blood of Jesus when consecrated by a priest during Mass. Unlike the ciborium, the chalice is never used to "store" the precious Blood in between Masses. Its contents are consumed immediately during Mass, and the chalice is carefully cleansed by the priest or deacon after the distribution of Holy Communion and kept ready for the next Mass.

- Paten: This round, flat, golden or silver-colored plate holds the large host that the priest consecrates during Mass. You will typically see it placed on top of the chalice beneath the chalice veil, before and after Mass. The paten can be thought to represent the manger in which the newborn Jesus was placed by his mother, Mary: "And she gave birth to her first-born son and wrapped him in swaddling cloths, and laid him in a manger, because there was no place for them in the inn" (Luke 2:7). The connections between the infancy of Jesus and the Eucharist are profound when you think about the paten. The French word *manger* means "to eat," and it was there, in Bethlehem, which in Hebrew means "House of Bread," that the baby Jesus was placed for the shepherds to see and adore when they visited.

- Cruets: These small glass bottles with stopper lids contain the wine and water used by the priest during Mass.

- Monstrance: The Lord in the Blessed Sacrament is exposed for adoration in this ornate metallic sacred vessel. It is often shaped like a stylized sun, symbolizing rays of light emanating from the center compartment, which contains the host behind clear glass, and it rests on a raised gold or silver base. The word monstrance derives from the Latin verb *monstrare*, which means "to show."

- Pyx: This small gold or silver metal container has been used in the Catholic Church since the earliest centuries as a safe way for a priest or deacon or even a layperson, under specific circumstances, to carry consecrated hosts to sick people, prisoners, or others who are unable to attend Mass. The word pyx comes from the Greek word *puxis* (πυξίς) for "box tree."

LITURGICAL VESTMENTS AND COLORS

One of the most noticeable features of the Catholic Mass is that the priest wears sacred vestments while ministering at the altar. These vestments are reserved for liturgical ceremonies—the most important being the Mass—and they signify the awesome duty entrusted to the priest to offer a sacrifice that is holy and pleasing in God's sight. The Bible tells us how the priests of the Old Covenant, who served in the temple, also wore special vestments.[3]

When serving at the altar, bishops priests, and deacons all wear a long, white garment called an "alb,"[4] symbolizing purity, chastity, and simplicity. This can be seen as a reminder of how dazzlingly white Christ's garments became on the Mount of Transfiguration,[5] as well as the biblical depictions of how God cleanses us[6] and the glorious white robes worn by the blessed in heaven, symbolic of their victory over sin and death.[7]

An ancient liturgical tradition in the West, which is still commonly honored, was for deacons, priests, and bishops to also wear a rope belt known as a "cincture"[8] around the waist. The cincture not only functioned as a practical way of keeping the alb in place, it also came to symbolize the many biblical commands to "gird" oneself in preparation for preaching, teaching, and other ministries.[9]

Over the alb, bishops and priests wear a "chasuble," and deacons traditionally wear a "dalmatic." The chasuble, from the Latin word "*casula*" (hut or little house), symbolizes that the priest has taken upon his shoulders the "yoke" which Jesus spoke of in Matthew 11:30. The deacon's outer vestment, the dalmatic, symbolizes his ministry of service at the altar. The word *dalmatic* itself derives from the region of Dalmatia (modern-day Croatia), where the custom of wearing it seems to have originated.

Bishops, priests, and deacons also wear a "stole," a long, narrow band of cloth that, for deacons, hangs over one shoulder and is fastened at the opposite hip, and for bishops and priests, is draped over both shoulders. The stole is symbolic of the role as shepherd that bishops and priests have in their ministry,[10] and it too, like the chasuble, is redolent of taking upon oneself the yoke of Jesus.

The colors of the vestments correspond to liturgical seasons (e.g., violet during Lent and Advent, white during the Easter season, and green during Ordinary Time) or to feast days.[11]

Because red symbolizes blood and fire, red vestments are worn on the feast days of martyrs, Palm Sunday, Pentecost, and Masses commemorating Jesus's passion and death. Black, traditionally the color of mourning in the West, is sometimes worn for funeral Masses. Rose, the color of joy, is worn on Gaudete Sunday (the third Sunday of Advent) and Laetare Sunday (the fourth Sunday of Lent) to remind us of the nearness of Christmas and Easter.

Sacramentals

Sacramentals are not sacraments, but they are means by which God bestows actual grace on his people. The *Catechism* defines sacramentals as

> sacred signs which bear a resemblance to the sacraments. They signify effects, particularly of a spiritual nature, which are obtained through the intercession of the Church. By them men are disposed to receive the chief effect of the sacraments, and various occasions in life are rendered holy. (*CCC* 1667)[12]

Sacramentals do not confer the grace of the Holy Spirit in the way that the sacraments do, but by the Church's prayer, they prepare us to receive grace and dispose us to cooperate with it:

For well-disposed members of the faithful, the liturgy of the sacraments and sacramentals sanctifies almost every event of their lives with the divine grace which flows from the Paschal mystery of the Passion, Death, and Resurrection of Christ. From this source all sacraments and sacramentals draw their power. There is scarcely any proper use of material things which cannot be thus directed toward the sanctification of men and the praise of God. (*CCC* 1670)

Sacramentals include a host of Catholic customs and pious practices, including:

- making the sign of the cross;
- genuflecting before the Blessed Sacrament (showing due reverence to the Lord in the tabernacle and on the altar);
- blessing ourselves with holy water (a reminder of our baptism);
- blessed palm branches (symbolic of the honor shown to Jesus by the fickle crowds in Jerusalem on Palm Sunday, the week before his Passion and death);
- altar candles and votive candles, which symbolize our prayers and, more importantly, the light of Christ (see John 1:1–9);
- blessed ashes imposed on our foreheads on Ash Wednesday—the tangible reminder of the words of God to Adam and Eve after the Fall: "Remember, man, that thou art dust and to dust thou shalt return" (see Genesis 3:19);
- incense, which represents our prayer rising in a sweet-smelling cloud before the throne of God (see Revelation 5:8, 8:3–5);
- pilgrimages (which allow Catholics to walk in the footsteps of Jesus, Mary, and the saints).

Crucifixes, statues, icons, and images are sacramentals that allow our minds to focus on the reality of Jesus, Mary, and the saints, who are in heaven but are invisible to our physical eyes. In the Catholic Church, the use of sacred images such as these is the equivalent of our having pictures of our family: the pictures represent the ones we love and long for.

Medals and scapulars are absolutely not meant to be thought of as magical or superstitious, but to remind us of God's love for us and our love for him and for Our Lady. Just as wearing a wedding ring doesn't make a person married, wearing a scapular or medal doesn't make a Catholic holy, but it does serve as a ready reminder of his commitment to a life of holiness and of his devotion to Jesus and Mary.

Another sacramental is the manger scene we display at Christmas. Developed by the great St. Francis of Assisi, the crèche offers us an image of the greatest love the world has ever known: Jesus Christ, the second Person of the Blessed Trinity, the Son of God, becoming human for our salvation. This sacramental goes hand in hand with the crucifix. In the former, we see the sweet baby Jesus coming to us in profound humility and tenderness; in the latter, we see his innocent flesh, scourged and torn and bleeding, crucified for our sins. We come full circle.

Fasting and abstinence are two more sacramentals integral to Catholic piety, as they are effective means for us to unite ourselves more closely with our Lord, who suffered for us. By denying ourselves certain pleasurable things, such as meat on Friday, we can make progress in subduing our unruly passions, do penance for our sins, intensify our will to be virtuous, and avoid sin in the future.

The Precepts of the Church

The *Catechism of the Catholic Church* explains the precepts of the Church (i.e., binding obligations on all Catholics) as follows:

> The precepts of the Church are set in the context of a moral life bound to and nourished by liturgical life. The obligatory

character of these positive laws decreed by the pastoral authorities is meant to guarantee to the faithful the very necessary minimum in the spirit of prayer and moral effort, in the growth in love of God and neighbor. (*CCC* 2041)

The precepts are these:

1. You shall attend Mass on Sundays and holy days of obligation and rest from servile labor.
2. You shall confess your sins at least once a year.
3. You shall receive the sacrament of the Eucharist at least during the Easter season.
4. You shall observe the days of fasting and abstinence established by the Church (i.e., fasting on Ash Wednesday and on Good Friday; abstinence from eating meat on those days and on all Fridays during Lent).
5. You shall help to provide for the needs of the Church.

THE CHURCH CALENDAR

Like the four seasons of nature, the liturgical calendar of the Catholic Church includes seasons for penance, celebration, and growing in holiness. The Church's "New Year" is the first Sunday in Advent. Both Advent and Lent, the periods of preparation before Christmas and Easter, are times of penance. They are followed by the joyful seasons of Christmas and Easter, times of rejoicing. The weeks between these seasons, which make up the longest part of the Church year, are known as Ordinary Time. Green vestments are worn during Ordinary Time to symbolize hope and growth, as Catholics focus on growing in faith and holiness.

In addition to seasons, through its liturgy, the Catholic Church delights in celebrating and commemorating the major episodes in the life of Christ (e.g., his birth, his resurrection, his Ascension), as well as feast days honoring the Blessed Virgin Mary and the saints, especially those men and women who were martyrs, doctors (i.e., teachers), and in other ways exemplars of Catholic holiness. A saint's feast day is usually celebrated not on his or her birthday, but on his or her "birthday into eternity"; that is, the day he or she departed to be with God in glory. It might also be considered the saint's "graduation day."

You will notice that the Church has a calendar of feasts. You can follow this calendar in the books known as the *Liturgy of the Hours* or even using your smartphone, your iPad, or your computer with an app such as iPieta. These resources let you enter into the spirit of these feast days by providing Bible readings for you to ponder as well as brief biographies about (and sometimes writings from) the saint honored on a given day.

The saints are living, breathing models of holiness for us, pointing the way toward our heavenly homeland and encouraging us by their prayers and good example. Ultimately, in all the saints, we really see Jesus Christ, the one whom they sought to emulate and follow.

> Therefore, since we are surrounded by so great a cloud of witnesses, let us also lay aside every weight, and sin which clings so closely, and let us run with perseverance the race that is set before us, looking to Jesus the pioneer and perfecter of our faith, who for the joy that was set before him endured the cross, despising the shame, and is seated at the right hand of the throne of God. (Hebrews 12:1–2)

Just as, at a natural level, people everywhere are keen on family togetherness and sharing good food on holidays, Catholics place an even greater importance on our family unity in the body of Christ. The holidays and feast days of the Church's liturgical calendar remind us of how important it is to join together as a Church (i.e., the Church triumphant, suffering, and militant) and celebrate with the heavenly bread of the Holy Eucharist, the victory won for us by Jesus Christ and our love and devotion to our Triune God, Father, Son, and Holy Ghost. We do this together at every Mass.

CHAPTER FIVE

WHEN IN DOUBT
Learn the Rules of Catholic Etiquette

WHEN YOU TAKE UP RESIDENCE IN A FOREIGN COUNTRY, THE TWO most important things to learn are the local language and the local customs. Without at least a working knowledge of both, it can be difficult to enjoy your new surroundings fully. It is crucial to understand what's considered appropriate and inappropriate, polite and offensive, if you want to make friends and have a happy, productive life in harmony with your neighbors.

Many books have been written explaining the fine details about how some innocuous gestures and social conventions in the United States are actually rude or even insulting in other countries. Take, for example, the American "A-OK" signal made by touching the tips of your index finger and thumb together to form a circle, or the thumbs-up ("everything's good") sign. Both are offensive in Turkey, Greece, and Middle Eastern countries. As you can imagine, understanding local customs is important!

Those coming into the Catholic Church need similar information to help them get their bearings and to become assimilated into their new culture. This chapter will examine some of the major forms of etiquette common in the Latin Rite of the Catholic Church in North America. Keep in mind that while a great deal of these Catholic culture norms are also the norm elsewhere in the world (e.g., in Europe and Latin America), there are still some variations, depending on where you live. The focus here will be on some of the major customs and forms of etiquette you'll see in the Catholic Church in the United States and Canada.

As the old saying goes, "When in Rome, do as the Romans do." Just so, when in the Catholic Church, do as the Catholics do.

THE SIGN OF THE CROSS

Perhaps the most visible indication that someone is Catholic is if he or she makes the sign of the cross. This holy gesture, in which we trace the sign of our salvation on our person and use the words Jesus gave us in the Great Commission (see Matthew 28:19–20)—"In the name of the Father and of the Son and of the Holy Spirit. [Amen]"—is intended to remind us of several things:

1. Our confidence in Jesus Christ, who conquered death and won eternal life for us by his Passion and death on the cross (see 1 Corinthians 1:17, 2:1–2; Galatians 6:14)

2. Our baptism, which was administered with the same words (see Matthew 28:19–20)

3. Our identity as sons and daughters of God the Father (see Ephesians 2:13–18; Colossians 1:19–20)

4. Our identity as Christians who, as Jesus commanded us, are resolved to pick up our cross daily and follow him (see Matthew 10:38, 16:24) on this earthly path to holiness and into eternity

5. The blessings of God that we invoke on ourselves and others each time we make the sign of the cross with prayerful, heartfelt reverence (see Galatians 3:14)

6. Our visible rejection of Satan and all his pomps and empty promises and the fact that, by dying on the cross, Jesus defeated Satan once and for all: On the cross, "He disarmed the principalities and powers and made a public example of them, triumphing over them in him" (Colossians 2:15)

7. A defense against demons, for by the power of the cross, "now shall
the ruler of this world [i.e., Satan] be cast out" (see John 12:31)

St. Cyril of Jerusalem says that the sign of the cross "is the sign of the
faithful and the terror of the demons, for the Lord triumphed over
them with this sign. Show it forth boldly, for seeing the cross they will
remember the crucifixion; they fear the one who crushed the head of
the dragon."[1]

DEVOTIONS

The Catholic Church is rich in spirituality and devotions, which include
the Stations of the Cross (in which we meditate on Jesus's Passion and
Crucifixion), the liturgical hours (different hours of the day dedicated
to special prayers and readings), blessing ourselves with holy water (a
reminder of our baptism), public Eucharistic processions (to live out St.
Paul's reminder in Romans 1:16 "not [to] be ashamed of the gospel"),
pilgrimages, May crownings (to honor the Blessed Virgin Mary), and
many others. These are all part of living a Catholic life and help us focus
our minds and hearts on God.

SIT, STAND, KNEEL

Newcomers to the Catholic Church are often surprised by how much
"up and down" there seems to be at Mass. It can be confusing if you
don't know the underlying reasons for sitting during some parts,
standing during others, and kneeling during others. First, the most
basic reason: We worship God "in spirit and truth" (John 4:24), yes,
but also with our bodies. Because we're composite beings made up of
body and soul, matter and spirit, we're able to show our love and adoration to God in both ways: spiritually, through our thoughts and mental
prayers, and physically, through our gestures (e.g., bowed head, folded
hands, raised hands), our voice (e.g., singing, vocal prayer), and our

posture (e.g., kneeling, bowing, standing). The various parts of the Mass that are differentiated by our sitting, standing, or kneeling are ways of expressing with our bodies truths about our relationship to God and our desire to worship him.

Perhaps you've wondered what it would have been like if you could have lived at the time of Jesus and have seen him in person. St. John Chrysostom, the fourth-century archbishop of Constantinople, understood this desire and reminds us that in the Holy Eucharist, we really do encounter Jesus: "Many people nowadays say, 'I wish I could see his shape, his appearance, his clothes, his sandals.' Well, look! You do see him, you touch him, you eat him."[2]

This real presence of Jesus in the Eucharist calls for reverence in our attitude and our posture. In the West, kneeling has long been the traditional Catholic custom for showing reverence to the Lord at Mass and in other liturgical settings. The most common form of respect is the genuflection—kneeling briefly on the right knee when passing in front of the tabernacle, in which Jesus is truly present in the Blessed Sacrament. It is a time-honored custom in the Western Catholic Church to genuflect when entering a pew in church, when approaching or passing in front of the tabernacle, and when leaving your pew.[3]

In the Eastern Catholic Church, the custom is to make a profound bow, something one should do when passing in front of the altar, the sacred table on which the Holy Sacrifice of the Mass is offered. We reverence the altar with a bow out of respect for the fact that it represents both the table at which Jesus and the apostles celebrated the Last Supper and the Cross on which the Lord was crucified, suffered, and died for our salvation.

Get into the habit of genuflecting whenever you pass in front of the tabernacle and—especially when the tabernacle is not in the center of the sanctuary but is off to one side—of bowing whenever you approach or pass in front of the altar.[4] You can never show too much respect to Jesus in the Blessed Sacrament.

Remember too that you yourself become a "living tabernacle" when you receive Jesus in Holy Communion, for he is truly present within you at that time.[5] This is why the ancient custom in the Catholic Church after receiving Holy Communion is to spend several minutes in intense, heartfelt prayer, offering gratitude, thanksgiving, and praise to God for this profound gift.

St. Maximilian Kolbe once wrote of Jesus in the Eucharist: "You come to me and unite yourself intimately to me under the form of nourishment. Your blood now runs in mine, your Soul, Incarnate God, compenetrates mine, giving courage and support. What miracles! Who would have ever imagined such!"[6]

You will usually see Catholics kneeling in the pew after receiving Holy Communion, heads bowed, deep in prayer. This, by the way, is why visiting, chitchatting, and doing anything other than focusing prayerfully on God during Mass, especially in those minutes just after Communion, while people are trying to make a good thanksgiving, is very inconsiderate to your neighbor and disrespectful to God.

Chitchat should take place outside or in the parish hall after Mass, not inside the church when people are trying to pray. As you have no doubt experienced, it is extremely distracting and difficult to pray when people around you are chattering away, seemingly oblivious to the fact that they are in the Lord's presence and are, in effect, ignoring him.

When you enter a church or a chapel and see the host exposed in a monstrance on the altar, such as for Eucharistic Adoration, it is customary to kneel on both knees—kind of a "two-knee genuflection"—and bow profoundly to the Lord before entering a pew and before you leave. This is not mandatory, however, and no one should look down on or scorn someone who does not kneel on both knees. Some sign of reverence is called for, though: a genuflection or, for those hampered by age or infirmity, bad knees, or some other physical problem, a profound bow or even just a reverent bow of your head, if that is all you are physically capable of doing.

God knows your heart. The important thing is to make a conscious sign of respect to the Lord. He, of course does not *need* this (though he certainly deserves it when you, a creature, come into the immediate presence of the Creator, the King of Kings, the God of the universe!), but you certainly do. It is very good for you to cultivate your love for him even in small ways such as showing reverence.

During Mass, there are certain times when we sit, stand, and kneel.[7] These posture changes are not arbitrary. The Catholic Church recognizes that we human beings can and need to express truths through our bodily postures.

We see in the Bible, for example, the story of the two sisters Mary and Martha, who were close friends of Jesus. While Martha was busy in the kitchen, tending to mundane things, Mary, we are told, was sitting at the Lord's feet pondering his teaching (see Luke 10:39–40). This is a biblical example of why we sit when the Word of God in Scripture is proclaimed and the bishop, priest, or deacon then expands on and explains the readings[8] in his homily.

Like Mary, we sit and ponder these divine truths during the first reading from the Old Testament, followed by the Psalm, followed by the second reading (on Sundays), and then we stand as a way to show special reverence for Jesus, whose person and teachings are proclaimed by the priest or deacon in the Gospel reading.

In the Latin Rite, we kneel at certain moments of the Mass, such as during the Eucharistic Prayer, to show our profound love and reverence for Jesus Christ and his sacrifice for us. Imagine yourself standing on Calvary at the foot of the cross as Jesus, shedding his precious blood for your sins, suffers in agony and eventually dies for you. Kneeling in reverence is a worthy, wholly appropriate posture in the presence of the Eucharistic Lord.

Standing, as the Blessed Virgin Mary, St. John, and the holy women did at the foot of the Cross, is also an appropriate posture, and this has since ancient times been the custom in the Eastern Church. These customs should be respected, each in its own context, especially because they preserve a long and indelible solidarity with the earliest Catholics, who also stood and knelt during the Mass.

The "universal norm" in the Latin Rite of the Catholic Church is to kneel for the consecration during Mass. In the United States, the long-standing custom, approved by the U.S. Catholic bishops, has been to kneel from the Sanctus (i.e., "Holy, Holy, Holy") until the Doxology ("Through him, with him, in him") at the end of the Eucharistic Prayer, just before the Our Father. The Church's *General Instruction for the Roman Missal* (GIRM) explains:

> A common bodily posture, to be observed by all those taking part, is a sign of the unity of the members of the Christian community gathered together for the Sacred Liturgy, for it expresses the intentions and spiritual attitude of the participants and also fosters them.
>
> The faithful should stand from the beginning of the Entrance Chant, or while the Priest approaches the altar, until the end of the Collect; for the Alleluia Chant before the Gospel; while the Gospel itself is proclaimed; during the Profession of Faith and the Universal Prayer; and from the invitation, Orate, fratres

(Pray, brethren), before the Prayer over the Offerings until the end of Mass, except at the places indicated here below.

The faithful should sit, on the other hand, during the readings before the Gospel and the Responsorial Psalm and for the Homily and during the Preparation of the Gifts at the Offertory; and, if appropriate, they may sit or kneel during the period of sacred silence after Communion.

In the Dioceses of the United States of America, they should kneel beginning after the singing or recitation of the Sanctus (Holy, Holy, Holy) until after the Amen of the Eucharistic Prayer, except when prevented on occasion by ill health, or for reasons of lack of space, of the large number of people present, or for another reasonable cause. However, those who do not kneel ought to make a profound bow when the Priest genuflects after the Consecration. The faithful kneel after the Agnus Dei (Lamb of God) unless the Diocesan Bishop determines otherwise.

For the sake of uniformity in gestures and bodily postures during one and the same celebration, the faithful should follow the instructions which the Deacon, a lay minister, or the Priest gives, according to what is laid down in the Missal.[9]

Pope Benedict XVI explained further why such traditional postures at Mass are so important and why they should be observed:

The Church's great liturgical tradition teaches us that fruitful participation in the liturgy requires that one be personally conformed to the mystery being celebrated, offering one's life to God in unity with the sacrifice of Christ for the salvation of the whole world. For this reason, the Synod of Bishops asked that the faithful be helped to make their interior dispositions correspond to their gestures and words. Otherwise, however carefully planned and executed our liturgies may be, they would risk falling into a certain ritualism. Hence the need to provide an education in Eucharistic faith capable of enabling the faithful to live personally what they celebrate....

A mystagogical catechesis must also be concerned with presenting the meaning of the signs contained in the rites. This is particularly important in a highly technological age like our own, which risks losing the ability to appreciate signs and symbols. More than simply conveying information, a myst-agogical catechesis should be capable of making the faithful more sensitive to the language of signs and gestures that, together with the word, make up the rite.[10]

Since the Catholic Church is a family, it might be helpful to consider these customs in light of the following hypothetical: Imagine you and your family have gathered together for Christmas dinner, and some people eat seated at the table, while others eat standing. That would be awkward and antithetical to togetherness and harmony.

Bishop Thomas Olmsted of Phoenix superbly encapsulated the reasons kneeling can be so spiritually beneficial to our participation in the Mass:

Knees symbolize both strength and humility. Athletes use strong knees to run for touchdowns in football and to block shots and to slam-dunk in basketball. Knees also bend in adoration of the Eucharistic King and in recognition of the grandeur and majesty of the Most High God. Already in Biblical times, knees were a symbol of humility and strength.

To bend one's knee before God was a profound act of worship; it stated boldly yet simply that God is the source of all power and that the one on bended knee is ready to place his life and all his energy at the service of the Lord.

What we do with our knees gives evidence of what we believe in our hearts. When we kneel down beside the bed of a dying person, when we stand up for the dignity of the unborn child, when we genuflect before Christ in the Blessed Sacrament, we say louder than any rhetoric what matters most in our lives.

Knees express what we believe and make clear what we will live and die for. Not surprisingly, then, knees play an important role in the Church's Sacred Liturgy, especially during the season of Lent. What we do with our knees during worship is anything but trivial. It rivals in importance what we do with our voices and our ears, what we do with our hands and our hearts.

When we gather at the Eucharist, our attention is drawn with awe and devotion to the sacramental presence of Christ. While the body of Christ far exceeds the value of our own bodies, it also gives meaning to them. It reminds us, too, of the human body's vital role in that "full, conscious and active participation in the Sacred Liturgy" called for by the Church at the Second Vatican Council.

It is understandable then why our posture at Holy Mass stirs such deep emotion within us who cherish our Catholic faith, and who know that our greatest treasure is the Eucharist. In three liturgical postures at Mass, our knees play a central role: kneeling, standing, and genuflecting.[11]

These postures remind us of our need for humility, for joy and exulta-tion, for contemplation and reverence, especially when we are in the presence of the Lord at Mass, but throughout the rest of our day-to-day lives as well.

TERMS OF ENDEARMENT (AND RESPECT)

Another item of Catholic etiquette is the ancient and universal custom of addressing priests as "Father." This is something St. Paul himself did and encouraged others to do:

> I am writing you this not to shame you, but to admonish you as my beloved children. Even if you should have countless guides to Christ, yet you do not have many fathers, *for I became your father in Christ Jesus through the gospel. Therefore, I urge you, be imitators of me.* (1 Corinthians 4:14–16, *NAB*, emphasis added)

St. Paul's advice to "be imitators of me" not only refers to his virtues and way of life, but includes calling him and the other priests of the Church "Father" out of recognition of their spiritual fatherhood. This dimension of the Catholic priesthood (which does not depend upon the personal qualities, likability, dedication, or virtue any given priest may have or not have) is manifested by the fatherly qualities inherent in the priestly ministry that parallel at the supernatural level those duties of our natural, earthly fathers. These include giving life by the regeneration of the soul (i.e., giving us new birth in Christ) that takes place through the sacrament of baptism (see John 3:3–5; Titus 3:5).

Priests, like earthly fathers, are also charged with dispensing the medicine we need to be cured when we are laid low by sin (see John 20:20–23; 2 Corinthians 6:18–20; James 5:13–16). And, most important of all, priests feed us in the Eucharist with the body, blood, soul, and divinity of Jesus Christ under the appearances of bread and wine (see 1 Corinthians 11:23–32).

Priests, like natural fathers, also give us counsel and encouragement to help us make tough decisions and bear life's difficulties. And just as any natural father, though not perfect—and perhaps far from perfect—can still give good advice and wise counsel (even if he could stand to take that advice himself), Catholic priests need not be perfect in order to guide us. Some priests are very virtuous and diligent in carrying out their priestly duties out of love for God and for the souls in their care. Some, maybe, not so much—though the great majority of priests are good men trying as best they can, with the help of God's grace, to carry out a demanding and often difficult ministry. So, whatever their personal flaws might be (let's not forget that we all have various flaws), calling them Father is a proper and biblically based custom that helps us remember the ministry to which our Lord has called these men.

Some argue that Christ's command in Matthew 23:9 (*NAB*), "Call no one on earth your father; you have but one Father in heaven," is sufficient proof that we should not call priests "Father." But this is actually a misreading of Christ's meaning. Jesus was here speaking against the scribes and Pharisees who, in various ways, tried to put themselves on such a high pedestal above the people that they actually sought to circumvent God's commandments!

One outrageous example of this was their so-called Korban rule, under which someone could shirk his responsibility to honor his father and mother (see Exodus 20:12), especially when they asked for financial help. The Korban tradition entailed the shell game of "donating" one's money to the temple so that, when the parental units asked for financial help, the son or daughter could say, "I'd like to help you, but I've already donated all my money to God." This was merely a ruse, though, because according to this scheme, the person still retained full control over all his money, even though he had technically "given it all to God." This clearly violated the fourth commandment ("Honor your father and mother"), and Jesus understandably condemned this practice as a corrupt tradition of corrupt men (see Matthew 15:1–9 and Mark 7:6–13).

This is an important biblical clue as to why calling priests Father does not conflict with Jesus's teaching in Matthew 23. Furthermore, we have the added testimony of the apostolic writers of the New Testament who routinely, and under the inspiration of the Holy Spirit, used the term "Father" as a religious title (see, for example, 1 Thessalonians 2:11 and 1 John 2:13–14).

St. Stephen, for example, who was the Church's first martyr, was "filled with the Holy Spirit," we're told in Acts 7, and he addressed the Jewish leaders who had plotted to kill Jesus as "my brothers and fathers." Clearly, since the Holy Spirit and Jesus can never be in conflict, nor could they contradict one another, the fact that the Holy Spirit inspired St. Stephen to address those religious leaders as "father" is itself sufficient to demonstrate that Jesus could not have meant literally in Matthew 23 not to use the word *father* when referring to or addressing certain men.

As we saw earlier, all Catholic clergy are in one of three levels of holy orders. The first and lowest is the diaconate. Permanent deacons are those who will not be ordained to a higher level. In the United States, it's quite common for a parish to have at least one permanent deacon assigned to it. Some parishes have five or six! Deacons are addressed and referred to as Deacon Michael or Deacon Jones and, in correspondence, Reverend Mr. Jones.

Priests, like deacons, are commonly referred to by first or last name: Father Dominic or Father McGillicuddy and, in correspondence, Rev. McGillicuddy.

Bishops are in the third and highest level of holy orders. It's most common to address a bishop more formally, using his last name—for example, Bishop Campbell—but a few bishops prefer to be addressed by their first name, such as Archbishop Seán (O'Malley), the cardinal archbishop of Boston. Since his being made a cardinal, he continued this custom, and everyone knows him as and addresses him as Cardinal Seán. It's a matter of personal preference.

As long as we're on the subject of bishops (also known as a group as the "episcopacy" or the "episcopate"),[12] let's note that the distinctions of honor that exist within these three levels of holy orders are purely a matter of custom, not doctrine, and are honorary in nature, usually designating a greater degree of responsibility in ministerial duties. Some priests receive the honorary title of Monsignor. And bishops can also be named archbishop as a designation of honor, or, more commonly, because the archdiocese they are appointed to lead is a large metropolitan see.[13]

The ecclesiastical title of "cardinal" (from *cardo*, the Latin word for "hinge") designates a man who has been entrusted with certain very important duties. You might say that some significant portion of the Catholic Church's work "hinges" on his leadership and supervision, including, most importantly for the life of the whole Church, the duty to meet in conclave and elect a new pope when one dies.

The office of cardinal is very ancient, going back to the Middle Ages, when certain prominent clergymen, including priests, were designated by the pope as having special authority to assist him in the governance of the Church, especially locally in the Archdiocese of Rome.

The pope is the bishop of Rome, but he is also the visible head of the Church on earth and, as a result, must attend to a vast global array of good works, projects, and problems, which means he needs more than a little help from the College of Cardinals to accomplish everything.

Pope Paul VI (1897–1978) set the upper limit for the total number of cardinals at 120, but any pope can modify this custom as he sees fit. The current rule is that only cardinals who are younger than eighty are eligible to vote in conclave to elect the next pope. Under the current *Code of Canon Law*, only men who are already ordained priests or bishops are qualified to be named cardinal.

A priest who is named a cardinal must be subsequently consecrated as a bishop, or, if he does not wish to do that, the pope can grant him a dispensation from this requirement. Recent recipients of such a dispensation were the American Cardinal Avery Dulles, S.J. (1918–2008) and the French Cardinal Yves Congar, O.P. (1904–1995), both of whom were important priest-theologians who wielded considerable influence in theological circles and were rewarded with this honor by St. John Paul II in thanks for their service to the Church.

"Have there ever been lay cardinals?" you ask. Well, yes and no. There were some men who had not yet been ordained even to the diaconate who were named cardinals by a pope. One notable example was Reginald Pole (1500–1558), an Englishman who was made a cardinal by Pope Paul III (1468–1549) even though he had not yet been ordained. However, though he had not yet received holy orders, he was still not technically a layman, because he was already installed in the clerical state, which until recently included the minor orders or ministries of porter, lector, exorcist, and acolyte.[14]

These minor orders (which have since been abolished) involved a special blessing and tonsure (i.e., having the crown of the head shaved, leaving a distinctive ring of hair to identify the man as a cleric), which was conferred by the pope on certain bishops who either oversee a prominent archdiocese (e.g., New York, Los Angeles, Chicago) or who don't run a diocese but do carry out important, high-level duties at the Vatican.

Stipends

A minor but ubiquitous part of Catholic etiquette is the stipend, or small cash donation often made to a priest in gratitude for his agreeing to celebrate an extra Mass or offer a regularly scheduled Mass for your special intention (e.g., for the repose of the soul of your recently deceased relative). In the United States, stipends offered for the celebration of Mass for a special intention are typically about ten dollars, though some Catholics, if blessed with more ample financial resources, give more. The Archdiocese of Atlanta recently published helpful guidelines for the offering of stipends, including the reminders:

> Mass stipends are offerings given by the faithful when they request that a Mass be offered for a specific intention. They are distinct from any gift that might be given to a visiting priest as an expression of thanks or as compensation for his time and travel.
>
> Only one stipend can be taken for each Mass, and the Mass must be offered for that intention, alone. A single intention may be for multiple individuals: e.g.: For the deceased members of the Knights of Columbus.... A priest should not refuse to offer a Mass because a small amount of money is offered for the stipend.[15]

Stipends are also customary for special celebrations such as weddings, baptisms, and funerals. Stipends are not mandatory, and no priest may ever refuse to provide you with the sacraments, such as baptizing your baby or burying your deceased relative, if you do not offer a stipend. To do so would be to commit the grave sin of simony,[16] which involves the "buying or selling of spiritual things," such as ecclesiastical offices and sacraments.[17] The *Catechism* says of this sin: "It is impossible to appropriate to oneself spiritual goods and behave toward them as their owner or master, for they have their source in God. One can receive them only from him, without payment" (*CCC* 2121). Canon lawyer Cathy Ciardi explains:

[To] many people it may seem crass for clerics to expect to receive monetary compensation for their ministerial activities. But at the same time, we all know that priests need sufficient income to cover their living expenses, just like the rest of us! Canon 281.1 notes that the clergy deserve appropriate remuneration, since they have dedicated their lives to spiritual ministry. And...[they] are not, as a rule, supposed to be engaged in trade or business outside of their ministerial assignment (cf. cc. 285 and 286). Consequently, if priests weren't compensated by the faithful in exchange for their spiritual ministrations, from what other source could they possibly derive a source of income?

In a typical first-world country today, parish priests receive a set salary. In some poorer nations, however, priests still depend on the stipends they receive for celebrating Masses, in order to support themselves. But regardless of each priest's actual need, canon 945.1 observes that every priest is allowed to accept a stipend for the celebration—or the concelebration—of a Mass. (See "Mass Intentions and Stipends" for a scenario involving the concelebration of one Mass by multiple priests.)

At the same time, there is another, spiritual component to the notion that the laity should give an amount of their own money in exchange for the sacramental ministry of a priest. Making an offering for (let's say) a wedding generally involves a financial sacrifice, much like almsgiving does—and as such it can be a meritorious act in itself. Additionally, the expense incurred also reminds us of the importance of the ministerial act that we are requesting. As human beings, we naturally tend to attach less value to things that we receive for free! Thus there is no intrinsic problem with the Church establishing a standard amount that is requested for the celebration of a Mass, or for a wedding, a baptism or other types of sacramental ministry by the clergy.[18]

THE IMPORTANT ROLE OF LAYPEOPLE

In its Dogmatic Constitution on the Church, *Lumen Gentium*, the Second Vatican Council emphasized the central importance of the role of laypeople in the Church, noting that, numerically, laypeople comprise by far the vast majority of the membership of the Catholic Church. Here are some of the highlights of this document's teaching on the role of laypeople as an important part of the Church:

> The laity are gathered together in the People of God and make up the body of Christ under one head. Whoever they are they are called upon, as living members, to expend all their energy for the growth of the Church and its continuous sanctification, since this very energy is a gift of the Creator and a blessing of the Redeemer.
>
> The lay apostolate, however, is a participation in the salvific mission of the Church itself. Through their baptism and confirmation all are commissioned to that apostolate by the Lord Himself. Moreover, by the sacraments, especially holy Eucharist, that charity toward God and man which is the soul of the apostolate is communicated and nourished. Now the laity are called in a special way to make the Church present

and operative in those places and circumstances where only through them can it become the salt of the earth. Thus every layman, in virtue of the very gifts bestowed upon him, is at the same time a witness and a living instrument of the mission of the Church itself "according to the measure of Christ's bestowal."

Besides this apostolate which certainly pertains to all Christians, the laity can also be called in various ways to a more direct form of cooperation in the apostolate of the Hierarchy [i.e., the bishops]. This was the way certain men and women assisted Paul the Apostle in spreading the Gospel, laboring much in the Lord. Further, they have the capacity to assume from the Hierarchy certain ecclesiastical functions, which are to be performed for a spiritual purpose.

Upon all the laity, therefore, rests the noble duty of working to extend the divine plan of salvation to all men of each epoch and in every land. Consequently, may every opportunity be given them so that, according to their abilities and the needs of the times, they may zealously participate in the saving work of the Church.[19]

These broad themes are explained in greater detail in the Council document on the role of the laity, *Apostolicam Actuositatem*.[20] It emphasizes that the role of laypeople consists primarily "in building up society whereby they strive to perform their domestic, social, and professional duties with such Christian generosity that their manner of acting should gradually penetrate the whole world of life and labor."[21]

Now that you're Catholic (and even if you're still on the journey home to the Church or have come home after a long absence or have been Catholic your whole life), never think that laypeople are second-class citizens or that you do not have an important role to play.[22] Just the opposite is true! The clergy have their special role to fulfill for the good of the body of Christ, including their mission to serve the lay faithful by administering the sacraments, celebrating Mass, preaching and teaching, and by their lives of charity and sacrifice for others giving witness to all that Jesus Christ has called us to follow him along the path to heaven, each person living out that call, whether married or single, lay or ordained.

CHAPTER SIX

When Storms Arise
Have Faith in the Church

As part of my work, I fly a lot, traveling to speaking events at universities, conferences, and parishes across the country and around the world. Most of the time, the weather's calm and the flights are smooth. Sometimes, though, when high winds and unstable air cause turbulence, a flight can become unpleasant. And then there are those rare but memorable flights that have been downright scary.

Flight attendants, who fly for a living, routinely experience bad weather, so they're used to it. They've been through it before, many times, and they know what to expect. That's why my policy is: if the flight attendants don't seem bothered by turbulence, then I won't be. But when they look concerned and nervous, I start to worry.

So consider a parallel with a biblical account of how Jesus calmed a storm. Imagine yourself with the apostles in the boat during that storm on Lake Galilee. Several of these burly guys are themselves professional fishermen. They've been through plenty of storms. They know from years of experience what to expect from the lake. Most of the time, when the wind and the waves kick up, they shrug and keep working. But this storm is bigger and more violent than anything they've encountered before. In fact, it's so bad that these experienced fishermen are seriously afraid they'll all drown.

> And when he got into the boat, his disciples followed him. And behold, there arose a great storm on the sea, so that the boat was being swamped by the waves; but he was asleep. And they went and woke him, saying, "Save [us], Lord; we are perishing." And he said to them, "Why are you afraid, O men of little faith?" Then he rose and rebuked the winds and the sea; and there was a great calm. And the men marveled, saying, "What sort of man is this, that even winds and sea obey him?" (Matthew 8:23–27)

That Jesus was asleep during this raging storm should tell us something. St. Mark's account of this incident includes the detail that the disciples shook Jesus awake, saying to him, "Teacher, do you not care if we perish?" (Mark 4:38). You can imagine the panic in their voices and the fear in their eyes as they waited to see what Jesus would do.

You and I are, if I can be forgiven for putting it this way, in the same boat as the disciples were on that stormy day. It can seem as if Jesus is asleep today, as the Catholic Church presses forward through the cyclones of life, buffeted, battered, and tossed around by the wind and the waves of this world, not to mention those churned up by apathetic, lukewarm, hypocritical, or wicked lay Catholics; priest sex scandals; negligent and self-indulgent bishops; media mockery; political harassment; and even bloody persecution. There are countless problems within and outside the Catholic Church that are as troubling as the gale the apostles feared would sink them on the lake.

Even so, the Lord's response to us today is the same, especially when our predicament looks hopeless and fear and panic threaten to plunge us under waves of despair: "Why are you afraid, O men of little faith?" In fact, he reminds us that "with men this is impossible, but with God all things are possible" (Matthew 19:26).

Let's keep these assurances in mind as we consider some of the challenges Catholics face nowadays.

British commentator Joanna Bogle, a Catholic convert from Anglicanism, wrote a very helpful little book called *Come On In, It's Awful!* In it she provides a fascinating history of the Catholic Church in England. As the title suggests, she explains how, even though the state of affairs in the Catholic Church can be difficult, messy, and confusing, it's still the Church Christ established, it's still where we belong, and in fact, the Church needs us to help clean things up and move things forward. This is something all baptized Catholics are called to take part in, given their time, temperament, and opportunities to do so.

Another way to express the circumstances the Catholic Church is in today—indeed, in which it always seems to be!—is the beginning of Charles Dickens's *A Tale of Two Cities*:

> It was the best of times, it was the worst of times, it was the age of wisdom, it was the age of foolishness, it was the epoch of belief, it was the epoch of incredulity, it was the season of light, it was the season of darkness, it was the spring of hope, it was the winter of despair.[1]

The same can be said about the Catholic Church you've come into (or back into). In it, you will find great saints and terrible sinners and everyone in between. Don't let that throw you. Part of the Church's role as a "sign of contradiction" (see Luke 2:33; Acts 28:22) involves its mixed composition of divine and human—a divine founder and head (Jesus) and a human membership. This is a mystery, yes, but one that Jesus himself predicted and even ordained to be so when said that the kingdom of heaven, the Church, is like a field of wheat and weeds (see Matthew 13:24–30). The field is the world, he says, and the crop originally planted in it is wheat. But an enemy sows weeds overnight, causing consternation among the workers whose job is to harvest the wheat. But rather than allowing the workers to pull up the weeds, the master says, "No; lest in gathering the weeds you root up the wheat along with them. Let both grow together until the harvest; and at harvest time I will tell the reapers, Gather the weeds first and bind them in bundles to be burned, but gather the wheat into my barn" (Matthew 13:29–30).

The particular type of weed Jesus mentions here is translated into English as either "tares" or "darnel," from the Greek word *zizanion* (ζιζάνιον).

Darnel is nearly indistinguishable from wheat and, as one scholar says, "usually grows in the same production zones as wheat and is considered a weed. The similarity between these two plants is so great that in some regions, darnel is referred to as "false wheat." It bears a close resemblance to wheat until the ear appears."[2]

One way to tell wheat from darnel is that the head on a wheat stalk droops (analogous to Christian humility), while the darnel plant stands up straight (analogous to stiff-necked pride).

You will encounter this phenomenon in the Catholic Church. It's not always apparent who is genuinely trying to practice the faith and be a dedicated disciple of Jesus and who is simply giving that appearance but inside is lukewarm or worse.

Don't let that throw you or discourage you. In fact, to change metaphors, take heart in Jesus's assurance: "I am the good shepherd; I know my own and my own know me" (John 10:14). Do your best to live your faith well, to love God and your neighbor, to trust in God's grace, and to move forward without worrying about the state of others' souls.

The Church in the World

Another way the Catholic Church is a sign of contradiction is that it is always and everywhere "spoken against," which is the literal meaning of the Greek word *antilegō* (ἀντιλέγω), used in Acts 28:22. By becoming

Catholic, you become one with Jesus Christ, about whom the prophet Simeon spoke when Mary and Joseph presented him in the temple as an infant: "Simeon blessed them and said to Mary his mother, 'Behold, this child is set for the fall and rising of many in Israel, and *for a sign that is spoken against*' [i.e., a sign of contradiction]" (Luke 2:34; emphasis added).

The Church, therefore, being the visible presence of Jesus on earth since his Ascension into heaven, has always been a lightning rod for opposition, just as Jesus was. From the very beginning, emperors, kings, despots, presidents, tyrants, dictators, politburos, and committees everywhere have tried strenuously not merely to "speak against" the Catholic Church but, if they had their way, to destroy it.

We have eyewitness accounts of this phenomenon. In the first century, for example, the Roman historian Publius Cornelius Tacitus (A.D. 56–117) described the diabolical lengths to which the evil emperor Nero went in his campaign to exterminate Christians as a way to deflect public suspicion from himself for having been responsible for the burning of Rome:

> [Nothing] availed Nero from the infamy of being believed to have ordered the conflagration. Hence, to suppress the rumor, he falsely charged with the guilt, and punished with the most exquisite tortures, the persons commonly called Christians, who were hated for their enormities. Christus, the founder of that name, was put to death as a criminal by Pontius Pilate, procurator of Judaea, in the reign of Tiberius, but the pernicious superstition, repressed for a time, broke out again, not only through Judaea, where the mischief originated, but through the city of Rome also, whither all things horrible and disgraceful flow from all quarters, as to a common receptacle, and where they are encouraged.

Accordingly first those were arrested who confessed they were Christians. Next, on their information, a vast multitude were convicted, not so much on the charge of burning the city, as of "hating the human race."

And in their deaths they were also made the subjects of sport, for they were covered with the hides of wild beasts, and worried to death by dogs, or nailed to crosses, or set fire to, and when the day declined, burned to serve for nocturnal lights.

Nero offered his own gardens for that spectacle, and exhibited a Circensian game, indiscriminately mingling with the common people in the habit [i.e., costume] of a charioteer, or else standing in his chariot. Whence a feeling of compassion arose towards the sufferers, though guilty and deserving to be made examples of by capital punishment, because they seemed not to be cut off for the public good, but were victims [of] the ferocity of one man.[3]

Now, try to picture yourself as Roman citizen at that time and in that place. You've been listening to St. Peter and St. Paul and their companions preaching the gospel of Jesus Christ throughout the city of Rome. You've been drawn to it, pulled in by the tug of truth and beauty. You're ready to seek baptism and entrance into the Catholic Church. And then this ferocious persecution against these very people breaks out in the most horrifying way! What do you do?

What a terrible time to convert, right? To say the least, you'd be asking for serious trouble with the government and very possibly death. These were the very questions people in those days had to ask themselves. And do you know what happened? The more the Church was persecuted, the more the floodgates of conversions opened.

The early Church historian Eusebius of Caesarea (c. A.D. 260–339) records in his *History of the Church* that the Church grew rapidly especially during times of bloody persecution. No matter how furious the onslaught of persecution, it was never anywhere near capable of suppressing, much less vanquishing, the Catholic Church.

We can take great consolation and encouragement from this fact of Catholic history that has repeated itself countless times over the last two thousand years. Today, in the twenty-first century, the Church remains, as ever, as sign of contradiction, both in its own composition of good and bad, saints and sinners, sheep and goats, wheat and weeds. It has always been thus. And, as ever, the world continues to speak against the teachings of the Church, seeking to convince us to go along to get along, to compromise and give in and, if at all possible, to depart from the teachings of Christ in the name of becoming up-to-date, sophisticated, reasonable, nonjudgmental, scientific, and tolerant.

This is particularly clear in the area of sexual morality. Just consider the full-court press the media is engaged in right now in an effort to paint anyone who adheres to traditional biblical principles of morality as hate-mongering, intolerant, homophobic, medieval, holier-than-thou bigots who seek nothing more than to impose their beliefs on others and force people to live according to their moral dictates.

"You can't force your opinions on me!" someone says.

"Why not?" you ask. "Are you saying I don't have a right to my own opinions?"

"No, you have a right to your own opinions, but you have no right to force your opinion on others."

"Oh. Is that your opinion?" you ask.

"Yes. That's my opinion."

"So then, why do you think it's okay to force your opinion on me?"

You can see the illogic of this situation. Moral relativism has made enormous inroads into our culture such that traditional standards of morality that were universally accepted as normal and sane are now regarded as extreme and outrageous and worthy of intense opposition in the name of tolerance. But notice that the Church hasn't changed its teachings; modern society has changed its attitudes on many moral issues, and now the Catholic Church is being painted as extreme.[4]

Catholic author Chris Stefanick points out why it is so important for Catholics, especially lay Catholics, to be ready, willing, and able to engage in thoughtful and friendly dialogue with those who have accepted and also promoted destructive ideologies such as moral relativism:

> Abortion was made legal by relativism and probably remains legal because of it. Though polls show a majority of Americans are opposed to abortion, they do nothing about it—most likely because a majority of Americans are relativists, not wanting to "impose their morality" on someone else. And so it seems that a multitude of Americans think an act is murder but won't do anything about it. This fact proves that we are able to turn a blind eye to any action of we think it falls under the protective umbrella of relativism. It isn't hard to see how this trend could be extremely dangerous.
>
> Thanks to relativism, our societal trend regarding human life won't end with legalized abortion. We are doing things today that humanity would have found almost universally repulsive until just a generation ago.[5]

This is yet another reason why it's important, now more than ever, for Catholics to see in the Church, as a sign of contradiction, their role to play in shining the light of truth in an ever-darkening world. We each have to do our part to live the truth, to speak the truth, and, should it be necessary, to suffer for the truth.

St. Paul put it succinctly in his encouragement to St. Timothy, a young bishop he appointed; it's advice we can all take to heart and seek to put into practice in our lives as Catholics:

> I charge you in the presence of God and of Christ Jesus who is to judge the living and the dead, and by his appearing and his kingdom: preach the word, be urgent in season and out of season, convince, rebuke, and exhort, be unfailing in patience and in teaching. For the time is coming when people will not endure sound teaching, but having itching ears they will accumulate for themselves teachers to suit their own likings, and will turn away from listening to the truth and wander into myths. As for you, always be steady, endure suffering, do the work of an evangelist, fulfil your ministry. (2 Timothy 4:1–5)

Our generation is not exempt from the trials and troubles that have beset the Catholics who have gone before us. Learning from their example, know that you can always call on God's grace and assistance as you do your best to speak the truth in love to a world that increasingly does not want to hear it.

Like the saints, we can be living icons of Christ and the Church as signs of contradiction by being charitable and friendly, patient and respectful, and, at the same time, uncompromising and clear in our beliefs and in how we share them with others.

Anytime you find yourself wondering, "Now what do I do as a Catholic?" just remember that Jesus talked about those who are wise and foolish. The "wise man," he says, is the one who "hears these words of mine and does them" (Matthew 7:24), likening this hearing and doing to building a house on rock, which cannot be dislodged or overcome, no matter how strong the wind and rain and flooding might get. This is the functional equivalent of standing firm on the rock of the Church and the teachings Jesus gives to make us truly free and happy.

Jesus also speaks about those who hear his words but do not do them. They, he says, are like those who attempt to build a house on the foundation of shifting sand. That house will fall, he says, "and great [will be] the fall of it" (see Matthew 7:27).

This is a great reminder for how important it is to engage culture from the standpoint of confidence born of the truth. Don't be afraid to speak the truth. Don't be afraid to live the truth. And never be afraid to stand up for the truth, even when it might mean suffering or even outright persecution. Just as the Church flourished in the early centuries because of the persecution inflicted upon it, so too will you become stronger and more joyful as a Catholic the more you become convinced of these truths and refuse to back down from them, come hell or high water.

Teach a Man to Fish
Living and Learning the Catholic Faith for Life

THE OLD ADAGE COMES TO MIND: "GIVE A MAN A FISH, FEED HIM FOR a day. Teach a man to fish, feed him for a lifetime." This can be a helpful way to think about your new life as a Catholic. It's one thing to have learned all the details of what it means to be Catholic—obviously things that are supremely important to know, but in themselves, those details are insufficient to sustain you throughout your life if they aren't put into practice.

It's kind of like the instruction manual in the glove compartment of your new car. It's good to know all those technical details about the car and where everything is located, but if you never actually drive the car and learn these things by using them, the manual doesn't do much good. It's there to get you started and, if you break down or a part goes bad, so you'll know how to fix things and get back out on the open road. In other words, now that you know the basics of the Catholic faith (or maybe even a great deal more than that), it's a matter of putting them into practice as you live out your Catholic identity. In this chapter we'll consider the primary ways you can do that.

Parish Life
The old saying, "No man is an island," is especially true when it comes to one's day-to-day life as a Catholic. By becoming a fully-fledged member of the Body of Christ through the sacraments of initiation (i.e., baptism, confirmation, and the Holy Eucharist) you belong in a very important

way to Christ and his Church, which you will experience, up close and personal, in your local parish church.

Your parish is where "the rubber meets the road" of your life in Christ. It's where (if I may be forgiven for mixing metaphors), you can turn on, tune in, and stay connected to Christ the Vine and all the other branches on the vine, so you can truly abide in him (see John 15:1–17).

Your parish is to your spiritual life what a hub is to a bicycle tire. Sunday Mass, the sacraments, other liturgical celebrations,[1] and regular, ongoing fellowship with other Catholics are like the spokes in the wheel. They connect the hub to the tire, keeping things straight, balanced, and road-worthy, no matter what debris, bumps, and sharp turns might lie ahead in this earthly life. Sunday Mass (even daily Mass, for those whose health and schedules allow them to avail themselves of that blessing) is central to your parish life. The more you plug-in at your parish by getting involved in activities and service (e.g., usher, greeter, lector, choir, Knights of Columbus, cleaning, food pantry, religious education, Bible study, etc.), the more you will personally grow as a Catholic *and* the more you can help others come to know and love Jesus Christ.

Your parish is the local expression of the Church universal *right where you are.* Be sure to register for collection envelopes so that you can participate in the ongoing support for the work of the Church locally. Your parish needs your financial support and envelopes are the best way to accomplish that. Of course, your pastor will likely not frown upon a one-time jumbo charitable gift if, say, you were to win the lottery. But since winning the lottery isn't very likely, the best thing to do is give as generously as you are able each week using your envelopes so you can help support all the many good works your parish undertakes to serve Catholics and non-Catholics alike.

Two other quick tips about parish life:

Pick up a copy of the bulletin and *read* it each week. The parish bulletin is a fantastic resource for staying plugged in to what's happening at the local level and around the diocese.[2] Many pastors include personal messages in the weekly bulletin, and you'll also find regular financial reports, announcements, and other resources. Ditto for your parish website.

If you're blessed to have Catholic radio in your area, another great way you can be of service to others is to help your pastor promote awareness throughout the parish and the wider community. See for example, Immaculate Heart Radio's suggestions on how to promote Catholic radio at your parish (www.ihradio.com).

In short, the stronger your connection to your parish and diocese, the deeper and stronger you'll become as a Christian, and the more greatly enriched as a person, besides.

A Life of Faith and Works

Jesus Christ is the foundation of your Catholic identity. You are building the temple of your soul on him, as St. Paul describes: "Do you not know that you are God's temple and that God's Spirit dwells in you?" (1 Corinthians 3:16).

The *Catechism of the Catholic Church* presents the entirety of the faith to us in four categories or "pillars," which we have considered in brief in this book thus far. They are:

- "The Profession of Faith" (i.e., the content of the Church's doctrines, or *what* we believe);
- "The Celebration of the Christian Mystery" (i.e., the Mass, the Holy Eucharist, and the sacraments, which comprise the liturgical expression of what we believe);

- "Life in Christ" (i.e., the moral life of a Catholic, learning to know what is true and do what is good, which is our exterior expression of what we believe through the virtues); and
- "Christian Prayer" (i.e., our ongoing dialogue with God and invocation of the Blessed Virgin Mary and the saints for their intercessory prayers, which is the interior expression of what we believe through prayer and other spiritual practices).

At a practical level, living the Catholic faith for life involves the daily combination of those last two things: doing good and speaking with God. Or, to say it in a more biblical way, faith and works. The combination of these two is the essence of a Catholic life well lived. Here's how St. John explains it:

> Beloved, if our hearts do not condemn us, we have confidence before God; and we receive from him whatever we ask, because we keep his commandments and do what pleases him. And this is his commandment: that we should believe in the name of his Son Jesus Christ and love one another, just as he has commanded us. All who keep his commandments abide in him, and he in them.... By this we know that we love the children of God, when we love God and obey his commandments. For this is the love of God, that we keep his commandments. (1 John 3:21–24, 5:2–3)

This is also known as the "obedience of faith" (Romans 1:5) or, "faith working through love" (Galatians 5:6). By it we live out our faith in Christ through what the Bible calls "good works." Doing good works cannot save us, but neither can faith alone. In fact, St. James emphasizes the need for the obedience of faith:

What does it profit, my brethren, if a man says he has faith but has not works? Can his faith save him? If a brother or sister is ill-clad and in lack of daily food, and one of you says to them, 'Go in peace, be warmed and filled,' without giving them the things needed for the body, what does it profit? So faith by itself, if it has no works, is dead.

But some one will say, 'You have faith and I have works.' Show me your faith apart from your works, and I by my works will show you my faith. You believe that God is one; you do well. Even the demons believe––and shudder. Do you want to be shown, you shallow man, that faith apart from works is barren? Was not Abraham our father justified by works, when he offered his son Isaac upon the altar? You see that faith was active along with his works, and faith was completed by works, and the scripture was fulfilled which says, "Abraham believed God, and it was reckoned to him as righteousness"; and he was called the friend of God. You see that a man is justified by works and not by faith alone.... For as the body apart from the spirit is dead, so faith apart from works is dead. (James 2:14–24, 26)

There are several important elements to notice here. First, St. James is speaking here about our saving justification by God's grace, not some notion of being "justified" (i.e., vindicated or proven correct) in the eyes of other human beings, as his example of Abraham and Isaac proves.

In Genesis 22, the passage in which we see the testing of Abraham when he was told by God to sacrifice his son Isaac, it says that when "Abraham lifted up his eyes and saw the place afar off," he "said to his young men, 'Stay here with the ass; I and the lad will go yonder and worship, and come again to you'" (Genesis 22:4–5). In other words, his justification which St. James invokes here, had no audience, the two helpers he brought with him having been ordered to remain at the foot of the mountain.

Second, though someone could claim he has faith, if that faith is not lived out in good works, in obedience to Christ, it is of no avail and cannot justify him; it cannot save him. As St. James says so plainly, "You see that a man is justified by works and *not* by faith alone," because "faith without works is dead." The converse is also true: works alone cannot save you, if they do not have the supernatural gift of faith. Just as there are those who imagine they can be saved by works alone, there are also many who think they will be saved by faith alone. Both notions are biblically incorrect. The truth, St. Paul says, is that:

> By *grace* you have been saved through faith; and this is not your own doing, it is the gift of God—not because of works, lest any man should boast. For we are his workmanship, created in Christ Jesus for good works, which God prepared beforehand, that we should walk in them." (Ephesians 2:8–10; emphasis added)

We are saved by grace alone. It's God's gift from beginning to end. And this grace enables us to have saving faith and to perform meritorious good works. We can neither boast about our works (God's gift) or about our faith (God's gift), and both go together. One without the other is useless.[3] This is why St. Paul is so emphatic about the role of works in justification in Romans 2.

But Jesus himself taught the same thing:

> Not every one who says to me, "Lord, Lord," shall enter the kingdom of heaven, but he who does the will of my Father who is in heaven.... Every one then who hears these words

of mine and does them will be like a wise man who built his house upon the rock;… And every one who hears these words of mine and does not do them will be like a foolish man who built his house upon the sand. (Matthew 7:21, 24, 26)

And behold, one came up to him, saying, "Teacher, what good deed must I do, to have eternal life?" And he said to him, "Why do you ask me about what is good? One there is who is good. If you would enter life, keep the commandments." He said to him, "Which?" And Jesus said, "You shall not kill, You shall not commit adultery, You shall not steal, You shall not bear false witness, Honor your father and mother, and, You shall love your neighbor as yourself." The young man said to him, "All these I have observed; what do I still lack?" Jesus said to him, "If you would be perfect, go, sell what you possess and give to the poor, and you will have treasure in heaven; and come, follow me." When the young man heard this he went away sorrowful; for he had great possessions. (Matthew 19:16–22)

When the Son of man comes in his glory, and all the angels with him, then he will sit on his glorious throne. Before him will be gathered all the nations, and he will separate them one from another as a shepherd separates the sheep from the goats, and he will place the sheep at his right hand, but the goats at the left. Then the King will say to those at his right hand, "Come, O blessed of my Father, inherit the kingdom prepared for you from the foundation of the world; for I was hungry and you gave me food, I was thirsty and you gave me drink, I was a stranger and you welcomed me, I was naked and you clothed me, I was sick and you visited me, I was in prison and you came to me." Then the righteous will answer him, "Lord, when did we see thee hungry and feed thee, or thirsty and give thee drink? And when did we see thee a stranger and welcome thee, or naked and clothe thee? And when did we see thee sick or in prison and visit thee?" And the King will answer them, "Truly, I say to you, as you did it to one of the least of these my brethren, you did it to me." (Matthew 25:31–40)

The point is, living a Catholic life isn't just about you and Jesus, as important as that relationship surely is. Because of your relationship with Jesus, it's important to branch out and love others for the sake of him, to become, wherever and whenever you find opportunities to do so (which is pretty much 24/7 for most of us) like the Good Samaritan who went far out of his way to rescue and care for a total stranger who really needed help.

You and I can do the same kind of thing, here and now, with the people we meet in daily life. It doesn't have to involve drama or special circumstances. It can be as simple as giving just having your radar up looking for ways to help those around you at work, in the grocery store, on the freeway, wherever you find yourself. Some real-life examples of this kind of everyday Good Samaritan come to mind.

One day, on my daily radio show,[4] a woman in San Diego called in to share a great idea she came up with to help the poor and homeless people in her area. She spends about an hour a week making up small personal kits consisting of a small, travel-sized toothbrush, toothpaste, comb, mouthwash, bar of soap, hand sanitizer, cotton washcloth, pack of tissues, lip balm, pen, notepad, chocolate bar, and a holy card with a picture of Jesus on it and a prayer on the other side. Each kit is contained in a plastic zipper bag to keep things dry. She keeps dozens of these inexpensive kits in her car and, when she sees a homeless person (often standing at street corners) she hands him or her a kit with a smile, showing the love of Jesus in a real, tangible, and meaningful way to someone who's likely alone, lonely, down on his luck, and afraid. This is beyond cool and is a perfectly doable way in which you can fulfill what St. Paul said in 1 Corinthians 10:24: "No one should seek his own advantage, but that of his neighbor" (*NAB*).

Another time, someone I know told me of his experience one evening in a grocery store, standing in line at the checkout. Ahead of him a woman in her mid-thirties with a couple of kids in tow was fumbling through her purse looking for cash after both her debit and credit cards had been declined.

She was flustered and embarrassed, and her kids were getting restless. Noticing her predicament, my friend smiled and with a cheerful, "I'll be happy to take care of that for you," handed the cashier a wad of twenties to cover the $100 total on the screen.

As you can imagine, the young mom was dumbfounded. Stammering, she at first declined to accept his generosity, no doubt abashed by the situation of being caught short of money, but my friend persisted assuring her it wasn't a problem and that others had helped him out of a jam before and this was an opportunity for him to give back.

Happy and shocked, she agreed to let him pay the tab but asked for his name and address so she could repay him. "God bless you, ma'am," he smiled as she wheeled the grocery cart and two kids away, a bewildered smile on her face. He had shared the love of Jesus with her in a way so unexpected that not only did she promptly send him a check to cover the total, she also sent a thoughtful, handwritten card with a message of heartfelt thanks. Only God knows what positive effects in someone's life acts of kindness and generosity like those can have on people.

OK, now here's the flip side of the coin.

Another friend of mine told me about a time he and his wife were having dinner on the outdoor patio of a restaurant. As they were eating their food and sipping their wine, they observed a homeless man rummaging for food in a dumpster next to a fast-food joint across the street. The wife put her fork down and exclaimed with concern about how hungry the man must be. The husband, glancing over at the homeless guy, didn't say anything and went back to his food.

"How sad!" his wife said with genuine concern. "That poor man! Just look at him. He must be really hungry if he's willing to dig for food in that nasty dumpster."

"He's probably just looking for food for his dog," my thick-skulled friend said offhandedly, not even looking up from his food, rationalizing away what was clearly a situation in which a fellow human being needed help.

My friend switched the subject and he and his wife finished their dinner, not giving the homeless guy across the street a second thought (at least my friend didn't). Later that night, when he knelt down to pray his evening prayers before bed, he experienced a real crisis of conscience.

His wife's comment—"He must really be hungry!"—clanged repeatedly in his mind like a dull, rusty gong. As he described it to me later, he suddenly felt weighed down by the crushing reality of how selfish, how callous, how lukewarm he had been back at the restaurant when he had in effect turned his back on the homeless man rather than acting, rather than getting out of his well-fed comfort zone and helping someone in need. Tears of sorrow and repentance ensued as he repented of not living his Catholic faith in a moment that was ready-made for a gesture of Christlike love.

His story made a deep impression on me. I confess that I myself have been in similar situations in which, right there in front of me, I've had a chance to do good for someone else but did nothing, out of fear, self-ishness, or just plain apathy and not wanting to be bothered. It was a powerful awakening for my friend when he realized he had turned his back on Jesus by ignoring that uncomfortable reality and passing up an opportunity to help someone who really needed help.

This episode is reminiscent of an incident in my own life that jolted me into realizing that, though Catholic in name, I had failed to live up to my calling as a follower of Jesus. One evening at dusk, on my way home from a long day at the office, I pulled into a gas station to refuel and grab a cup of coffee for the drive home. As I strode toward the mini-mart's glass door, a young man who was maybe twenty years old stepped tentatively toward me from out of the shadow between the ice machine and the trashcan. His voice faltering, he almost whispered, "Please, sir…" We locked eyes for an instant, and I sized him up before glancing away.

I knew instantly he meant no harm. Ragged and dirty, he seemed kind of scared, almost as if he were about to cry. Ashamed of begging. "Please, sir… I'm…"

"Sorry," I snapped, lips pressed tight as I stepped past him. I poured myself a nice, steaming cup of coffee and then flipped a $50 bill on the counter, telling the clerk, "I'll take this, and give me the change in gas on pump 7."

"I hope that guy's not still there," I thought to myself as I went back out, and grimaced slightly when I saw him still there, back in the shadows next to the ice machine. I pretended not to notice him as I pumped the gas, trying to put it out of my mind. Back in my car, I pulled out of the gas station parking lot and, just as I started to sip my coffee, an inky explosion of guilt and regret burst in my conscience. My mind wasn't blown. My soul was. I realized all in an instant what a self-satisfied, self-sufficient, *selfish* jerk I was by ignoring that young man and his genuine appeal for help.

Comfortable car with a full gas tank? Check. Toasty cup of fresh-brewed coffee to drink at my leisure? Check. Decent clothes? A job paying a decent salary? A comfortable home stocked with food and other amenities? A bed with fresh linens to sleep in that night and a clean shower in which to refresh myself? Check. Check. Check. Check. Check.

I hit the brakes and made a U-turn. Getting out of my car, I headed toward the young man, who was still hunched in shadows. Again, I saw that look of fear and hopelessness on his face and, this time, maybe even alarm as he saw me approaching, not knowing what my intentions might be.

"I'm sorry." I said, shaking my head in shame, fumbling with my wallet, not quite able to make eye contact. "I'm sorry I didn't help you." Grabbing the cash I had left in my wallet, I stepped toward him and said again, "I'm sorry," and handed him a wad of bills, maybe forty dollars. I don't know, because I didn't count them or stay to talk. Turning away in shame, I walked back to my car and drove off into the night.

"Thank you, sir!" he called out to me as I walked away, head down. "God bless you." Talk about a divine smack on the forehead. I've never forgotten that encounter or how it changed me. That young man was like a mirror. In him, God revealed my selfishness and showed me how, though I could talk a good game about being a follower of Jesus, when it came down to actually doing some of the things Jesus commanded (you know, like feeding the hungry, giving drink to the thirsty, clothing the naked, welcoming the stranger, etc.), I was a failure in many ways.

This auspicious encounter changed me by making me more aware that living my Catholic faith isn't something I just do for an hour a week on Sunday. It's not like a club I belong to or a hobby I practice when I feel like it or a trait I am known for and only practice when I think someone is looking. No. Being Catholic, I discovered painfully that evening, is an identity—something I (and you) should always be seeking after. I'm grateful to that young man standing in the shadows of the mini-mart that day. Maybe he was Jesus. No, he *was* Jesus. Of that I feel sure.

We all find ourselves in similar crossroads in daily life, quite often, in fact, for those who have eyes to see and ears to hear. Perhaps you've been reminded just now of comparable situations in your own life. If so, that's good! Whether you're a new Catholic or someone who's been in the Church for many years, you, like the rest of us, need to be reminded (even if forcefully) what being Catholic is really all about. Simply put, it's about Jesus's teaching, "If you love me, you will keep my commandments," he said (John 14:15). And what exactly is that commandment?

> And one of them, a lawyer, asked him a question, to test him. "Teacher, which is the great commandment in the law?" And he said to him, "You shall love the Lord your God with all your heart, and with all your soul, and with all your mind. This is the great and first commandment. And a second is like it, you shall love your neighbor as yourself. On these two commandments depend all the law and the prophets." (Matthew 22:35–40)

The key is to be actively, consciously, looking for opportunities to help others, spiritually as well as materially. As St. James reminds us:

> If a brother or sister is ill-clad and in lack of daily food, and one of you says to them, "Go in peace, be warmed and filled," without giving them the things needed for the body, what does it profit? (James 2:15–16)

You see, living out this call to help others doesn't require dramatic or grandiose gestures—in fact, they are spiritually counterproductive for you. Remember what Jesus said about this:

> Beware of practicing your piety before men in order to be seen by them; for then you will have no reward from your Father who is in heaven.
>
> Thus, when you give alms, sound no trumpet before you, as the hypocrites do in the synagogues and in the streets, that they may be praised by men. Truly, I say to you, they have received their reward. But when you give alms, do not let your left hand know what your right hand is doing, so that your alms may be in secret; and your Father who sees in secret will reward you. (Matthew 6:1–4)

The Bible also says, "Let brotherly love continue. Do not neglect to show hospitality to strangers, for thereby some have entertained angels unawares" (Hebrews 13:1–2). Not only do you not know how your sincere and selfless acts of charity can positively impact others, you also have no idea the blessings God wishes to pour out upon you as part of his plan for your life. Sometimes (maybe even more often than not), all that stands in the way of your receiving some beautiful and life-changing blessing from God is your own "yes" to a seemingly chance opportunity too good for someone else.

Whether it's volunteering at a soup kitchen, a community food pantry, a pro-life pregnancy office, or a similar community outreach, you can take an active part in living your Catholic faith in powerful ways by radiating the love of God through your everyday activities. Each time you open your heart to God's grace by loving others through service, almsgiving, a kind word, or even just a smile, you've made room for God's blessing in that person's life and also in your own. And, seriously, who among us couldn't use more blessings?

When Jesus said, "If you love me, you will keep my commandments" (John 14:15), he wasn't just talking about the Ten Commandments and their prescription for virtuous moral behavior. He also had in mind the commandments to love your neighbor as yourself. And this commandment extends even to those who not only aren't very loveable, but those as well who might well reject your kindness and repay you with ingratitude, or even anger. Even they, Jesus says, should be included in your efforts to radiate the love of Christ to those around you. You just never know what the results will be. And don't forget that these acts of kindness are as much for you and your growth in the virtues as they are for those you encounter. Consider these teachings about the importance of living your life in service to others:

> A new commandment I give to you, that you love one another; even as I have loved you, that you also love one another. By this all men will know that you are my disciples, if you have love for one another. (John 13:34–35)

> This is my commandment, that you love one another as I have loved you. Greater love has no man than this that a man lay down his life for his friends. You are my friends if you do what I command you.… This I command you, to love one another. (John 15:12–14, 17)

> On the subject of mutual charity you have no need for anyone to write you, for you yourselves have been taught by God to love one another.… Nevertheless, we urge you, brothers, to progress even more. (1 Thessalonians 4:9–10, *NAB*)

> Encourage one another, and build one another up.… We urge you, brothers, admonish the idle, cheer the fainthearted, support the weak…always seek what is good [both] for each

other and for all (1 Thessalonians 5:11, 14–15, *NAB*; see also 2 Corinthians 1:10–11)

"Man Does Not Live by Bread Alone"

Satan hassled and harassed Jesus with many different temptations during the Lord's forty-day desert fast before commencing his public ministry.

> And the tempter came and said to him, "If you are the Son of God, command these stones to become loaves of bread." But he answered, "It is written, 'Man shall not live by bread alone, but by every word that proceeds from the mouth of God.'" (Matthew 4:3–4)

Just as it is important to look after our neighbor's physical welfare, it's just as important to try to help him or her spiritually too. We don't require "bread alone," but also the food of truth and goodness that God imparts to us through divine revelation and the sacraments, beginning with the Holy Eucharist. One primary way we live out this dimension of the Catholic life is through intercessory prayer for others.

Christ commands us to "love one another." We should do this both physically, by helping others with food, shelter, and so on (see Matthew 25:31–46; James 2:14–17), as well as spiritually, by praying for them and showing a good example.

St. Paul reminds that we should always pray, supplicate, petition, and offer thanksgivings for everyone, because doing so is good and pleasing to God our savior (see 1 Timothy 2:1–4). Consider these related passages that teach the same thing:

> I urge you, [brothers,] by our Lord Jesus Christ and by the love of the Spirit, to join me in the struggle by your prayers to God on my behalf. (Romans 15:30, *NAB*)

In him [Jesus] we have put our hope [that] he will also rescue us again, as you help us with prayer. (2 Corinthians 1:10–11. *NAB*)

We always give thanks to God, the Father of our Lord Jesus Christ, when we pray for you.... We do not cease praying for you and asking that you may be filled with the knowledge of his will through all spiritual wisdom and understanding to live in a manner worthy of the Lord. (Colossians 1:3, 9–10, *NAB*)[5]

ALMSGIVING

Helping others financially is another important dimension of the Catholic life. There are a variety of ways to carry out this part of serving your neighbor. Here are some Bible verses that underscore why it's so important:

Give alms from your possessions to all who live uprightly, and do not let your eye begrudge the gift when you make it. Do not turn your face away from any poor man, and the face of God will not be turned away from you. If you have many possessions, make your gift from them in proportion; if few, do not be afraid to give according to the little you have. So you will be laying up a good treasure for yourself against the day of necessity. For charity delivers from death and keeps you from entering the darkness; and for all who practice it charity is an excellent offering in the presence of the Most High. (Tobit 4:7–11)

Sell your possessions, and give alms; provide yourselves with purses that do not grow old, with a treasure in the heavens that does not fail, where no thief approaches and no moth destroys. For where your treasure is, there will your heart be also. (Luke 12:33–34)

He who supplies seed to the sower and bread for food will supply and multiply your resources and increase the harvest of your righteousness. You will be enriched in every way for great generosity, which through us will produce thanksgiving to God; for the rendering of this service not only supplies the wants of the saints but also overflows in many thanksgivings to God. (2 Corinthians 9:10–12)

As for the rich in this world, charge them not to be haughty, nor to set their hopes on uncertain riches but on God who richly furnishes us with everything to enjoy. They are to do good, to be rich in good deeds, liberal and generous, thus laying up for themselves a good foundation for the future, so that they may take hold of the life which is life indeed. (1 Timothy 6:17–19)

Do not neglect to do good and to share what you have, for such sacrifices are pleasing to God. (Hebrews 13:16)

The Souls in Purgatory

Keeping in mind what we've already seen from St. Paul's teaching in 1 Corinthians 3, that the souls in purgatory—"the Church suffering"— are temporarily delayed in their entrance into heaven due to their need for purification and cleansing from the "wood, hay, and straw" that is incompatible with an all-holy God, let's now consider how living your Catholic faith involves helping these souls with your prayers and suffrages.[6]

Revelation 21:27 says that "nothing unclean shall enter" heaven. Therefore, since many people who die in the state of grace and are destined for heaven, nonetheless, have some "clean-up work" to take care of, it is part of the Christian life here on earth to pray for them.

Jesus alluded to this when he described a certain wedding feast that is symbolic of heaven. A guest appears at the feast without the required "wedding garment" and the king asks him, "'Friend, how did you get in here without a wedding garment?' And he was speechless. Then the king said to the attendants, 'Bind him hand and foot, and cast him into the outer darkness; there men will weep and gnash their teeth.' For many are called, but few are chosen" (Matthew 22:12–14).

Similarly, when someone departs from this life and isn't fully purified and, therefore, is unable to enter into the beatific vision, we can help him or her with our prayers that the Lord would hasten the purification necessary for him to go to heaven.

Don't forget this important aspect of your new life as a Catholic. The souls who are in purgatory now will eventually be in heaven, and they won't forget your kindness to them. In fact, they will repay you many times over with their own prayers for you.

The early Church Fathers testify to this biblical doctrine of purgatory and how you as a Catholic can help your brothers and sisters who are there by your prayers. For example, St. Cyril of Jerusalem declared:

> "[W]e make mention [at Mass] also of those who have already fallen asleep: first, the patriarchs, prophets, apostles, and martyrs, that through their prayers and supplications God would receive our petition; next, we make mention also of the holy fathers and bishops who have already fallen asleep, and, to put it simply, of all among us who have already fallen asleep, for we believe that it will be of very great benefit to the souls of those for whom the petition is carried up, while this holy and most solemn sacrifice is laid out."[7]

St. John Chrysostom also testifies to this great truth:

> Let us help and commemorate them. If Job's sons were puri-fied by their father's sacrifice, why would we doubt that our

offerings for the dead bring them some consolation? Let us not hesitate to help those who have died and to offer our prayers for them.[8]

Weep for those who die in their wealth and who with all their wealth prepared no consolation for their own souls, who had the power to wash away their sins and did not will to do it. Let us weep for them, let us assist them to the extent of our ability, let us think of some assistance for them, small as it may be, yet let us somehow assist them. But how, and in what way? By praying for them and by entreating others to pray for them, by constantly giving alms to the poor on their behalf. Not in vain was it decreed by the apostles that in the awesome mysteries remembrance should be made of the departed. They knew that here there was much gain for them, much benefit. When the entire people stands with hands uplifted, a priestly assembly, and that awesome sacrificial Victim is laid out, how, when we are calling upon God, should we not succeed in their defense? But this is done for those who have departed in the faith, while even the catechumens are not reckoned as worthy of this consolation, but are deprived of every means of assistance except one. And what is that? We may give alms to the poor on their behalf.[9]

St. Augustine too, among all the other Church Fathers, testifies to the importance of remembering in prayer the holy souls in purgatory. Here are several examples of his teaching on this important subject:

Temporal punishments are suffered by some in this life only, by some after death, by some both here and hereafter, but all of them before that last and strictest judgment. But not all who suffer temporal punishments after death will come to eternal punishments, which are to follow after that judgment.[10]

That there should be some fire even after this life is not incredible, and it can be inquired into and either be discovered or left hidden whether some of the faithful may be saved, some more slowly and some more quickly in the greater or lesser degree in which they loved the good things that perish, through a certain purgatorial fire.[11]

During the time, moreover, which intervenes between a man's death and the final resurrection, the soul dwells in a hidden retreat, where it enjoys rest or suffers affliction just in proportion to the merit it has earned by the life which it led on earth.

Nor can it be denied that the souls of the dead are benefited by the piety of their living friends, who offer the sacrifice of the Mediator, or give alms in the church on their behalf. But these services are of advantage only to those who during their lives have earned such merit, that services of this kind can help them. For there is a manner of life which is neither so good as not to require these services after death, nor so bad that such services are of no avail after death.[12]

As St. Paul explains in 1 Corinthians 3:10–15, the purification that happens in purgatory may well be in store for those Catholics who coast through life and don't really make much of an effort to let the grace of God transform them. But it doesn't have to. In fact, our goal should always be to strive to live a life worthy of the Lord's saying to you at the end of your life, "Well done, good and faithful servant; you have been faithful over a little…now enter into the joy of your Master" (Matthew 25:21).

YES, LIVING A HOLY LIFE IS EASIER SAID THAN DONE, BUT IT'S CERTAINLY not impossible. In fact, Jesus promises you all the grace and divine help you need to accomplish this goal.

The alternative to the abundant life in Christ is grim: mediocrity, dull, wishy-washy Christianity that is as selfish as it is purposeless. That wide and well-travelled road leads to eternal separation from God. Don't allow yourself to get back on it!

One effective way to do this is to frequently remind yourself that the devil wants nothing more than to keep you distracted and distressed, discontent and disillusioned, disengaged and disgruntled, and most of all, discouraged.

Satan offers only cheap, fake imitations of God's gifts: pleasure instead of happiness, entertainment instead of peace, part instead of whole, temporary instead of permanent, counterfeit instead of real. He's a liar, a cheater, a conman, a charlatan, a rip-off artist, a scammer. Don't let him scam you!

As a Catholic, you have at your fingertips all the divinely instituted, grace-filled tools necessary to defeat the devil's schemes. Rely on God's loving providence and entrust yourself to his grace so that you can spend the rest of your life laughing in the face of the devil's bogus claims. Those who let themselves get taken in by his get-rich-quick sales pitch will lose, every time.

Now is the time to make firm your resolution to stay close to God, standing on that rock upon which Christ is building his Church. As he promised, if you're on that rock, when the winds and the rain and the floods burst against that house, it will not fall because it has been built on a solid and unshakable foundation of Jesus Christ in his Church. A flimsy foundation of sand is the only alternative.

Consider his answer to the apostles' question, "Who then can be saved?" after listening to his dialogue with the rich young man who asked Jesus, "Now what?" In other words, "Now that I've gotten to this point, having kept the commandments, what should I do now?" (see Matthew 19:16–30; Mark 10:17–31).

The Lord answers his "Now what?" with an intriguing "Come and see" (John 1:39).

It is an invitation to something more, something better, brighter, greater, and higher than anything the world, the flesh, and the devil could possibly offer. Sadly, Scripture says the young man did not accept the invitation and "went away sad," never to be heard from again.

Don't be like him.

"Come and see" is the Lord's answer to your own "Now what?"

Now it's time to begin in earnest your exploration of his magnificent promises.

CHAPTER ONE

1. These are enumerated in the U.S. Constitution, which contains amendments known as the Bill of Rights.

2. *Code of Canon Law* (Washington, D.C.: Canon Law Society of America, 1983).

3. In the United States, the holy days of obligation are: the solemnity of Mary, the Mother of God (January 1); the solemnity of the Ascension (celebrated forty days after Easter or on the following Sunday, depending on the diocese); the solemnity of the Assumption of Mary (August 15); All Saints' Day (November 1); the solemnity of the Immaculate Conception (December 8); and Christmas (December 25).

4. Related to the Sunday obligation is the duty to attend Mass on all holy days of obligation, unless prevented by extenuating circumstances.

5. Tithing (i.e., giving 10 percent of one's income) is by no means required of any Catholic, nor does the Catholic Church impose any specific assessment regarding financial responsibility. Rather, the Church encourages generosity and leaves it up to the prayerful prudential judgment of each Catholic as to how much he wishes to donate to the work of the Church. The Archdiocese of St. Louis has prepared some helpful guidelines regarding donations, available at http://archstl.org/stewardship/page/faqs-about-tithing.

6. This is not to say that all Catholics actually put this into practice, or at least not as well as we can and should, but it certainly is the ideal to which Jesus calls all Catholics to strive for.

7. For anyone wanting to dive deep into the issue of how the human mind works, I recommend starting with Frank Sheed's legendary *Theology and Sanity* (San Francisco: Ignatius, 1993), pp. 21–76, and then graduating to John F. Wippel's *The Metaphysical Thought of Thomas Aquinas: From Finite Being to Uncreated Being* (Washington, D.C.: Catholic University of America Press, 2000).

8. See Pope Paul VI's landmark encyclical *Humanae Vitae* for the specifics. Listen also to Dr. Janet Smith's talk "Contraception: Why Not?" (available at www.janetsmith.org). And the book, *Adam, Eve, and the Pill*, by Mary Ebertstadt (Ignatius), is also quite helpful in making this case.

9. Plato (c. 428–348 B.C.), *The Republic*, book 7, in *Plato: Complete Works*, ed. John M. Cooper (Indianapolis: Hacket, 1997), pp. 1132–1155.

10. Plato, pp. 1133–1134.

11. In *Theology and Sanity* (San Francisco: Ignatius, 1993), Frank Sheed provides a penetrating and illuminating explanation of this sublime mystery of the Faith,

demonstrating that a mystery is not something we can know *nothing* about, it is something we cannot know *everything* about.

12. This last example, commonly called "the problem of evil," has been convincingly explained and resolved in books such as Peter Kreeft's *Making Sense Out of Suffering* (Cincinnati: Servant, 1986) and *Handbook of Catholic Apologetics* (San Francisco: Ignatius, 2009), and C.S. Lewis's *The Problem of Pain* (New York: HarperOne, 2009).

CHAPTER TWO

1. This, of course, is what is so frightening and unnatural about death, the separation of the body and the soul. Even so, because of Jesus Christ's decisive victory over death, when the general judgment takes place at the end of time, we will all, whether blessed or damned, experience the permanent reunification of body and soul for all eternity.

2. *Summa Theologiae*, III, Q. 60.

3. Fr. James T. O'Connor provides a helpful explanation in his superb book (which I encourage you to read) *The Hidden Manna: A Theology of the Eucharist* (San Francisco: Ignatius, 1988).

4. Pope John Paul II, *Dies Domini*, 30.

5. Some "high-church" groups within Lutheranism do, as do some Anglicans and a few others, though, numerically, they are small in number compared with the majority of Protestants.

6. See also Ezekiel 36:25; Matthew 3:13; John 4:2; 1 Corinthians 6:11.

7. C.S. Lewis, *Mere Christianity* in *The Complete C.S. Lewis* (San Francisco: HarperSanFrancisco, 2002), p. 23.

8. See 2 Chronicles 7:14; Ezekiel 33:11; Luke 13:3; Acts 3:19.

9. Related sections in the *Catechism*: 1113–1134, 1135–1666.

10. That is, the Blessed Virgin Mary who, by God's singular gift, was preserved free from original sin and from all actual sin from the moment of her Immaculate Conception onward (see Pope Pius IX's encyclical letter *Ineffabilis Deus*).

11. Pope Urban IV, *Transiturus*, 1264, quoted in James T. O'Connor, *The Hidden Manna: A Theology of the Eucharist* (San Francisco: Ignatius, 1988), pp. 192–196.

12. See also: Matthew 15:32–39 and Mark 8:1–9.

13. *Evangelium Vitae*, 43.

CHAPTER THREE

1. *Redemptoris Mater*, 1.

2. *Redemptoris Mater*, 6.

3. Pope Pius XII, *Mystici Corporis Christi*, 68, 74.
4. *Mystici Corporis Christi*, 62.
5. *Catechetical Lectures* III:3 (c. A.D. 350).
6. Pope Paul VI, Apostolic Constitution *Indulgentiarum Doctrina*, January 1, 1967, quoted in Patrick Madrid, *Any Friend of God's Is a Friend of Mine* (San Diego: Basilica, 1997).
7. Karl Adam, *The Spirit of Catholicism*, trans. Dom Justin McCann, O.S.B., rev. ed. (Garden City, N.Y.: Doubleday Image, 1954), p. 127.

CHAPTER FOUR

1. William Congreve, *The Mourning Bride* (1697).
2. Metal chalices are traditionally by far the most common form, but occasionally you will see some made of different material, such as stone or ceramic.
3. For a fascinating description of the Old Testament priestly vestments, see Alfred Edersheim, *The Temple: Its Mysteries and Services as They Were at the Time of Christ* (Grand Rapids: Eerdmans, 1990), pp. 96–100.
4. From *alba*, the Latin word for "white."
5. See Luke 9:27–36.
6. See Psalm 51:7 and Isaiah 1:18.
7. See Revelation 7:9–10.
8. From the Latin word *cingulum*, meaning "sword belt" or "girdle."
9. See Jeremiah 1:17; Job 38:3; 1 Peter 1:13.
10. Prior to the liturgical reforms of the Second Vatican Council (1962–1965), there were several additional vestments worn by the priest at Mass, including the amice, maniple, and biretta. You will see them when attending Mass in the Extraordinary Form, also known as the Traditional Latin Mass, which was the form of the Holy Sacrifice of the Mass that the great majority of priests in the Roman Rite of the Catholic Church celebrated from the late fourth century until Vatican II. Other liturgical rites within the Roman Rite included the Mozarabic, Sarum, Dominican, and Ambrosian rites, all of which were very similar in their major elements to the Latin Mass, which was codified at the Council of Trent (1545–1563) and commonly known henceforth as the "Tridentine Mass."
11. The color of the chalice veil and certain other altar cloths correspond to the color of the priest's vestments.
12. *SC* 60; cf. CIC, can. 1166; CCEO, can. 867.

CHAPTER FIVE

1. St. Francis de Sales, *The Sign of the Cross* (Manchester, N.H.: Sophia Institute, 2014), p. 81.
2. St. John Chrysostom, *Homily 82 on Matthew*.

3. This custom is so ingrained in lifelong Catholics (as well it should be) that more than a few of us have been abashed when, out of habit, we've genuflected absentmindedly upon entering a row of seats at the movie theater!

4. The use of tabernacles in the Catholic Church dates back to at least the middle of the fourth century, and became commonplace in the decades immediately after the legalization of the Catholic Church by the Roman emperor Constantine in the early 300s. For well over a millennium, the traditional location for the tabernacle in both the West and the East in the Catholic Church has been in the center on the back wall (the reredos) behind the altar or in a locked cabinet set into the wall on the right or left side of the altar. This became the preferred place of honor for the tabernacle once it became customary to reserve the Blessed Sacrament in a church or chapel.

5. The real presence of Christ in the Eucharist remains for as long as the host you received retains the properties of bread. The Church does not designate any exact length of time for this, though the generally accepted view is that the Lord remains present in the consecrated host, after it is consumed by the communicant, for at least the next five to ten minutes. Once the host has been swallowed and the bodily processes of emulsification and digestion take over, the real presence ceases.

6. Quoted in Regis J. Armstrong et al., *The Franciscan Tradition* (Collegeville, Minn.: Liturgical, 2010), p. 51.

7. The norms for when to stand, sit, and kneel during Mass are given in the *General Instruction for the Roman Missal*, an authoritative liturgical document issued by the Catholic bishops of the United States, available at http://www.usccb.org/prayer-and-worship/the-mass/general-instruction-of-the-roman-missal/index.cfm.

8. Since the Second Vatican Council, the Catholic Church has observed a three-year cycle of readings from the Bible for Sunday Mass and a two-year cycle for daily Mass. This enables Catholics to read and hear proclaimed a vast amount of the Bible over the course of three years. Catholics who pay attention to and internalize these biblical readings actually know far more Scripture than they may realize!

9. *The General Instruction of the Roman Missal*. Even though a few Catholics, including priests, deacons, and laypeople, insist that standing is preferable during those parts of the Mass when the Church's universal norms call for kneeling, it's important to note that, in this, they are out of step with the clear teaching of the Second Vatican Council, which emphasized that, "no other person, even if he be a priest, may add, remove, or change anything in the liturgy on his own authority" (*Sacrosanctum Concilium*, 3).

10. *Sacramentum Caritatis*, 64.

11. Bishop Thomas J. Olmsted, "Knees to Love Christ," *The Catholic Sun*, February 17, 2005, http://ewtn.com/library/bishops/kneeslov.htm.

12. The words *bishop*, *episcopacy*, and *episcopate* all derive from the compound Greek word *epi-skopos*, meaning "overseer." *Epi* means "above" or "over," and *skopeo* means "to see."

13. *See* is the English word derived from the Latin *sedes*, meaning "chair," "seat," "place," or "residence," as the "county seat" as the official administrative center for local government.

14. In 1972, Pope Paul VI revised the Church's laws regarding the minor orders (see his motu proprio *Ministeriam Quaedam*), suppressing the levels of exorcist and porter, as well as subdeacon, while retaining lector and acolyte but now referring to them as ministries rather than minor orders. Since this change took effect, the Catholic Church recognizes that the clerical state begins with ordination to the diaconate.

15. "Guidelines on Mass Stipends in the Archdiocese of Atlanta," February 5, 2010, http://www.archatl.com/offices/chancellor/docs/stipend-guidelines.pdf.

16. Named after Simon the Magician, who had the dubious distinction of trying to purchase with cash the office of apostle. You can read about his disastrous scheme in Acts 8:9–24.

17. The Catholic Church's *Code of Canon Law* lays out the rules regarding the giving and receiving of stipends: http://www.vatican.va/archive/ENG1104/_P3D.HTM.

18. Cathy Caridi, "Stipends and Sacraments," Canon Law Made Easy (blog), November 7, 2013, http://canonlawmadeeasy.com/2013/11/07/stipends-and-sacraments.

19. *Lumen Gentium*, 33.

20. The Latin title *Apostolicam Actuositatem* is the first part of the first sentence, which reads in English: "To intensify the apostolic activity of the people of God."

21. *Apostolicam Actuositatem*, 13.

22. Another resource to that will allow you to appreciate fully all the things laypeople are called to do in the Church is Cardinal Francis Arinze's book *The Layperson's Distinctive Role* (San Francisco: Ignatius, 2013).

CHAPTER SIX

1. Charles Dickens, *A Tale of Two Cities*: (Clayton, Del.: Prestwick, 2005), p. 9.

2. Craig S. Keener, *The Gospel of Matthew: A Socio-Rhetorical Commentary* (Grand Rapids: Eerdmans, 2009), pp. 386–387.

3. David Alphonso Talboys, trans., *The Annals and History of Tacitus* (London: Oxford, 1839), pp. 362–363.

4. Two very helpful books on refuting moral relativism are Peter Kreeft, *A Refutation of Moral Relativism: Interviews with an Absolutist* (San Francisco: Ignatius, 1999), and Francis J. Beckwith and Gregory Koukl, *Relativism: Feet Firmly Planted in Mid-Air* (Grand Rapids: Baker, 1998).

5. *Absolute Relativism: The New Dictatorship and What to Do about It* (San Diego: Catholic Answers, 2011), pp. 22–23.

CHAPTER SEVEN

1. Such as Eucharistic Adoration, vespers, Stations of the Cross, Marian processions, and the like.

2. A diocese, headed by a bishop or archbishop, is a territory that encompasses many parishes. Some dioceses are small, others massively large, but all of them are shepherded by a bishop, who has the responsibility of caring for the spiritual wellbeing of all Catholics in the diocese. As of this writing, there are approximately 195 dioceses in the United States and 72 in Canada.

3. At the Council of Trent (session VI), the Catholic Church reiterated its constant teaching that we are saved by grace alone, not by faith alone or works alone.

4. Heard Monday through Friday at 6:00–9:00 A.M. PST on more than 200 AM and FM stations across the U.S., as well as on Sirius Satellite Radio (channel 130). See www.patrickmadrid.com/patrick.

5. See also Matthew 5:42–46, 19:19; Mark 12:28–14; Luke 6:27–36; Romans 10:1, 12:9–13; Galatians 5:9–13, 6:2; Ephesians 4:4, 32; 1 Thessalonians 3:12, 4:9–10, 18; 2 Timothy 1:3; Hebrews 3:13; 1 John 4:7–21. See also, the *Catechism of the Catholic Church* (CCC 1822–1829, 1965–1974, 2093–2094).

6. The term *suffrage* does not mean "suffering"; it does not mean that one suffers here on earth for the souls in purgatory. Rather, *suffrage* refers to the ability of Catholics to offer up to the Lord our meritorious (i.e., done in grace) good works and intercessory prayers on behalf of those in purgatory (see 2 Timothy 1:18). See also 2 Maccabees 12: 43–45; Luke 16:19–31; 1 Corinthians 11:27–32; Hebrews 11:13–16, 32–40; 1 Peter 3:18–19, 4:6; CCC 1030–1032, 1472–1477.

7. *Catechetical Lectures* 23:5:9; A.D. 350.

8. Homilies on 1 Corinthians 41:5 (A.D. 392) (cited in the *Catechism of the Catholic Church*, 1032).

9. Third Homily on Philippians (A.D. 402).

10. *The City of God* 21:13 (A.D. 419).

11. *Handbook on Faith, Hope, and Charity,* 69 (A.D. 421).

12. *Handbook on Faith, Hope, and Charity,* 109.

ABOUT THE AUTHOR

Patrick Madrid is a bestselling author of more than eighteen books on Catholic themes. These include *Does the Bible Really Say That?*, *150 Bible Verses Every Catholic Should Know*, *Envoy for Christ: 25 Years as a Catholic Apologist*, and *On a Mission: Lessons from St. Francis de Sales*. He hosts a daily radio show, which is broadcast weekdays over the EWTN Catholic radio network as well as on Sirius Satellite radio.